NOBODY

NOBODY

or

The Disgospel According to Maria Dementnaya

NIKTO
(A Samizdat Text)

Translated from the Russian, with an introduction by

April FitzLyon

JOHN CALDER

LONDON

First published by Possev Verlag, Frankfurt-am-Main
First published in Great Britain 1975
by John Calder (Publishers) Ltd
18 Brewer Street, London W1R 4AS

ISBN 0 7145 0975 2   Casebound edition

Typeset in 11 on 12 point Pilgrim
Printed by Clarke, Doble & Brendon Ltd, Plymouth

CONTENTS

Introduction

Nobody first appeared in *samizdat*, the clandestine system by which home-made books—manuscripts and typescripts—pass from hand to hand within the Soviet Union. *Samizdat* is the only system of publication there which is free from state control, and is therefore the only source of free Russian literature within Russia. The manuscript of *Nobody* (dated 1966) somehow reached the West, and the novel was first published (in Russian) in the periodical *Grani*.[1] An anonymous French translation appeared in 1973.[2] The present translation is the first to appear in English.

It will be clear to anyone reading *Nobody* that it could never have been published by an official Soviet publishing-house. Its criticism of the Soviet régime is both

[1] *Grani*, No. 82, pp. 3–91, (Frankfurt-am-Main) December, 1971.
[2] *Nikto* (Denoël, Paris) 1973.

implicit and explicit; and everything else in the book—its philosophy, subject matter and literary style—is diametrically opposed to the tenets of Marxism and Socialist Realism which govern all Soviet publications and state-approved literature. The author is anonymous; partly, perhaps, because the fact that the hero becomes "nobody" is of prime importance in the novel; but also because if the author were known he would almost certainly suffer persecution at the hands of the Soviet authorities. Not that he reveals any damaging *facts* in his book as, for example, Solzhenitsyn does in *Gulag Archipelago*. *Nobody* is concerned with ideas, not facts; it contains no descriptions of physical horrors, such as torture or concentration camps. The horrors in this book are the horrors of the mind.

We know nothing about the author, except what we can deduce from his book: he is a very accomplished and sophisticated writer, of great originality—by Soviet standards, of startling originality; he is extremely well-read, familiar not only with Russian literature, but also with the Classics and western European literature, including authors not easily available in the USSR, and he also appears to have some knowledge of Japanese literature; he is familiar with the Gospels, with Cabbalistic writings, perhaps also with oriental philosophy; he is obviously familiar with the language of ancient mythology, with symbols; and he is, above all, a deeply religious man. He writes for an equally sophisticated and well-read audience—presumably, for his friends.

Nobody is a novel which can be read on several different levels. On the simplest level, it is a novel of alienation, the story of a Soviet *Steppenwolf*, told in a mixture of reality and fantasy, interspersed with occasional passages of black humour and satire directed against the Soviet régime, and with philosophical musings about the fate of Russia. On this level alone *Nobody* is something of a *tour de force*: it is a deeply tragic book which also succeeds in being extremely funny. The Ministry of Applause, for example, is hilarious satire, rather in the style of Ilf and Petrov; 'Dinner with the Family' is a wonderfully comic interlude which succeeds in highlighting the tragedy.

Novels of alienation have become something of a cliché in the West of recent years; in the Soviet Union, on the other hand, the whole problem of alienation is officially considered as inapplicable to Soviet reality, and can only be seen as a totally reprehensible state of mind. The pressure to conform in the USSR is far greater than it is in the western democracies, and the penalties for not conforming are greater too; for the Soviet citizen the question of conforming or not conforming is sometimes literally a question of life and death.

However, although *Nobody* does refer specifically to the predicament of the individual in the Soviet Union, much of the book could be equally true of the predicament of the individual in any other modern society. The differences between a Communist and a non-Communist society are, of course, fundamental; despite the many shortcomings of western capitalism, for example, we fortunately cannot yet echo Petatorov's bitter statement: "I would take my pen—and it would automatically write lying words! And no one believed them, because they were printed in Russia and their author was not in prison." Yet there are still many problems in the modern world common to individuals in both societies. Like Petatorov's friends and acquaintances, we too try to escape from reality by drinking, collecting things, reading poetry or pornography. We too compromise with our consciences, as the journalist Velzin does. We too have an Alternative Society, although not for the same reasons. In many passages in *Nobody* the author has succeeded in making the particular general; he has been able to transcend national and political differences and to bridge the gap between East and West, speaking for many people on both sides of the Iron Curtain.

However, important though the theme of alienation is in this book, and although the author's condemnation of the Soviet régime is bitter and explicit, it seems to me that these are not the most important aspects of *Nobody*. On the deepest level, it is concerned not so much with man's relationship to society, as with his relationship to himself—and to God. Gradually the meaning of the sub-title: "The Disgospel according to Maria Dementnaya" becomes a little clearer. The English word "disgospel" is, of course, a fabrication, as is the Russian word "disangeliye". If "gospel" means "good news", what then does "disgospel" mean? The reader must judge. But what is apparent from the text is that *Nobody* is indeed, in parts, a modern and abbreviated version of the story of the Passion.

Petatorov, the hero, certainly identifies himself with Christ. Does the anonymous author also identify his hero with Christ? This is much less clear. Petatorov sometimes uses Christ's words ("Watch with me,") or paraphrases them. He becomes "a wooden Christ, taken off a cross in a church"; he falls "cross-shaped" in the snow. It does also seem, from small details widely separated in the text, that Petatorov's birthday—and his spiritual rebirth—is on Christmas Day. Then, at the end of Chapter 7, Petatorov says: "What day is it tomorrow? *Thursday*." (The italics are the author's.) From then on, certain events of the Passion—the Mocking of Christ, the Agony in the Garden, the draught of vinegar, the Crucifixion itself (on Friday)—are sketched in in modern terms. The novel ends with Petatorov's death—there is, it seems, no Resurrection; but, despite his fearful sufferings, after death Petatorov has "a happy smile" on his face. We recall an earlier passage in the book, when he says to his friend: "The frail strings will snap and—it is the end, death . . . However, it is perhaps just at that point that the wild beast will be purified, by death and blood, and become a human being." The name of Petatorov's wife, Nadezhda, means "hope" in Russian, and this is clearly what she symbolizes in the book. But she is equally clearly identified with death. Must we then assume that hope and death are synonymous?

Petatorov's frequent assertions that "God is dead" do not seem to derive from Nietzsche. His ideas are, perhaps, closer to those of certain modern radical Christian theologians, such as the Americans Thomas Altizer and William Hamilton. The "Death of God" controversy was widely discussed in the west in the 1960s[1] when *Nobody* was written. It is unlikely, however, that literature concerning this controversy was easily available to Soviet citizens. For Petatorov, there used to be a God, Who has died or been killed. But, although he states that God is dead, in the same breath Petatorov says: "God is in me," or "What is God? A frame of mind—goodness." And, in an important passage, he says: "Men had a God, and He was chopped up on the executioner's block, everyone got a little bit: a quarter of an ear, a bit of finger nail or a slice of heart". However, later on in the cemetery Petatorov tells the old man: "I can't believe even in God. I did try . . . but nothing came of it." Religious philosophers will, no doubt, have their own solutions to the problems posed by these passages.

The ideas expressed by the old man in the cemetery derive directly from Jewish mysticism, the Cabbala, as

[1] See, for example: Thomas W. Ogletree, *The 'Death of God' Controversy*, (London) 1966.

does the language he uses.[1] Petatorov neither accepts nor rejects these ideas.

The use of symbols, which plays such an important part in this book, will not be lost on those interested in such things; and it is clear that the author uses symbols with a full knowledge of their ancient and universal significance. Whereas the meaning of *Petatorov's Dream* and *The Parable of the Chest* will probably be fairly obvious to everyone, *The Legend of the Black Panther* can, and no doubt will, be interpreted in many different ways. It is neither a dream, nor a parable, but a legend; in it we enter the realm of mythology, and its inner meaning will only be clear to those who can interpret the symbols.

The translator can do no more than offer some very tentative suggestions concerning the interpretation of this beautiful legend. In almost all mythologies winged creatures and birds symbolize spiritualization, higher states of being, the soul. The ornithologist, therefore, would seem to represent someone specializing in spiritual questions, perhaps a priest. The panther (or leopard) in ancient Egyptian and Indian mythology, symbolized the Watcher, God. Later, the Cabbalists sometimes referred to Jesus as *ben Panthira*; this relates to various legends which describe Jesus as the son (or grandson) of a man called Panthira, which may perhaps be a reminiscence— conscious or subconscious—of the panther's ancient symbolic meaning. It has also sometimes been suggested that the word "panther" derives from the Greek words *pan* and *theos*—although this seems highly improbable etymologically—meaning "all gods".[2] The white marking "like a noose" on the black panther could have many different

---

[1] See, for example: G. G. Scholem, *Major Trends in Jewish Mysticism* (London, 1955), p. 217
[2] See, for example: Harold Bayley, *The Lost Language of Symbolism* (London, 1951), Vol. I, pp. 84–5.

meanings; but the coupling of white with black is always significant, and gods and goddesses have often been depicted as half-white, half-black. Sometimes white signified time, while black signified eternity; but many other interpretations could be postulated.

If the panther be taken to symbolize God, this legend may relate to Petatorov's earlier description of the death of God: "Men had a God, and He was chopped up on the executioner's block, everyone got a little bit . . ." The ornithologist, it will be recalled, is still holding the panther's paws, which have been cut off, when he is taken away "to the proper place"—in other words, to the lunatic asylum. But these suggestions are, I repeat, very tentative, and others, no doubt, will have different solutions to offer.

In this marvellously concise novel few details are gratuitous or insignificant, although their meaning is not always immediately apparent. As in a musical composition, themes are enunciated, dropped, then reiterated and developed many bars later. There are passages of pure lyricism; and passages of complicated counterpoint, such as the scene on the railway-station. There are *Leitmotifs*: the old women, who seem to represent "straight" society, the silent majority (but why do they lisp and speak with foreign accents?); the old man in his bath, who marks the time people spend with Shulyatko in what is probably the Lubyanka (headquarters of the secret police). And what is the significance of the talking cat? It appears at first to be merely a piece of whimsy; but since Petatorov rejects a relatively easy death solely for the cat's sake, it is, perhaps, not quite as simple as that.

Names, too, are significant. Minuctov and Molierov

seem to be merely jokes; but Sabretooth-Sorbonne, in a passage in which mice and teeth play so prominent a part, is clearly more than a joke. It has been suggested[1] that Petatorov's patronymic Philip Arkadyevich—Philip son of Arcady—may have some significance; if this is so, has his friend Sheptunov's name Yuli Adamovich—Julius son of Adam—some significance too? The meaning of the names Maria Dementnaya and Libertova will be obvious to western readers; but they would only be obvious to Russian readers with a knowledge of Latin or of a Latin language, since the words for "demented" and "liberty" in Russian have quite different, non-Latin roots.

Nobody is firmly based in the Russian literary tradition. The author's debt to Gogol and Dostoyevsky is obvious; there are also similarities with the work of Mikhail Bulgakov. Above all, the Russian tradition of using literature as a vehicle for important social, political, philosophical and religious ideas is here closely followed —and for the traditional reason: the lack of a free press in Russia.

In *Petatorov's Dream* the author, in a striking image, describes hot, red blood flowing from the wounds made by the soldiers in Pushkin's bronze statue, while everyone in the crowd around is frozen dead. Can we interpret this as meaning that, in spite of every kind of repression, in spite of public apathy and indifference, the spirit of Russian literature alone is still alive? In any case, *Nobody* presents striking evidence that this is indeed true.

April FitzLyon

[1] By the anonymous French translator and, following him, by Jean Mambrino in ' "La mauvaise nouvelle" de l'homme souterrain' in *Etudes* (Paris) March, 1974, pp. 391–403.

Chapter 1

Petatorov's Day-dreams

Petatorov was freezing.

Autumn was over, the frosts had come; ice covered the asphalt, and all the same it was damp. Petatorov touched his face—cold and moist. Flags above the houses did not stir and hung down in a heavy mass, like skinned calves. Street-lamps droned and buzzed. Ahead at the cross-roads the shadow of a man appeared for a moment —and then once more only the frost made itself felt. The Sokolniki district of Moscow was going to sleep, amidst warmth and odours. Petatorov was hurrying. He had to go along two more side streets and almost the whole length of the Novooslepenskiy blind alley, and then he too would be in the warm. He was slightly worried that he hadn't paid for his room for two months; would his few things be lying outside in the little yard? He had not been back to his lodgings for a week, he had been roaming about, in and around the city; but now the frost was driving him back to his own warm lair, where he could lie on the old spring mattress, smoke, think of eternity, and drink cheap port.

"Ugh! How cold it is!"

In the spring Petatorov had ripped out the lining of his coat, and his landlady had made him some new trousers. The cloth of the sleeves had worn thin to the point of non-existence in places. His greasy jacket under his coat did not keep him warm at all.

I suppose I must have gone down hill a lot. Last summer I met someone I knew on the Arbat and looked the other way. I can't stand any of them, and I heard how they said compassionately behind my back "How low he's sunk!"

Did I ever really look any different! . . .

For all of them the most important thing is to "look". "How low he's sunk!"

Hm! And you think you have gone up in the world, do you? Falcons! Soaring up in the skies, you kites!

Philip Arkadyevich Petatorov had once been a learned philologist, had written articles, and even books. It must have been about four years since he had woken up one morning and suddenly felt bored. Heavens! I've lived for thirty whole years, and all to no avail. The blue bird is still uncaught, it's only in the Moscow Arts Theatre that it trustingly surrenders into your hands.[1] A century has passed, and every evening a bored actor catches a bored blue bird. Petatorov remembered how twenty years ago he happened to go to the theatre, and how a pensioner sitting in front had begun to weep, and

[1] A reference to Maeterlinck's play *L'oiseau bleu*, which has been in the repertoire of the Moscow Arts Theatre since 1908. The blue bird symbolizes happiness (*Tr. note*).

through his tears and snot had shouted: "Let me have it too! Let me have it too!" He had gone on banging his stick on the ground and shouting until they took him out. Oh yes, Petatorov was tired of it all, and he had left home. They must have tried to find him, he had seen his wife and son. They had wept, but he had sat there unmoved and bored. They had almost locked him up in a lunatic asylum. Probably the professor has fallen in love, they thought; his first professorial love will pass—and he'll come back, where else could he go? But they were wrong . . .

Petatorov was running along the street—I think it's—yes, here it is.

He opened the door and went through the kitchen, which was getting cold, to his own room.

"I really could devour something," thought the lecturer in philology.

His landlady shuffled out, panting, and said in a braying voice:

"It does seem a long time since we've seen you, Phil—It must have been before the October holidays you went away."

"I was busy, Gran. Here, take twenty roubles, I'll owe you the rest."

"You've become careless, Phil. For a whole year you were good about paying, but now—it's when you feel like it. And I have such a hard time! My pension—pooh! it's just enough for firewood, and that has to be fetched and sawn up. Ah, Phil!"

"When I start working, I'll give you six months' in advance," the lecturer promised, locking the door of his room.

"Will you really, Phil?!" fussed the landlady.

Petatorov heard the old lady go out into the corridor, and groan for a long time, feebly and voluptuously, in the lavatory. Then she switched off the light with a click and murmuring "Lord have mercy upon us miserable sinners," went back to her room.

"Miaou!" said the cat sleepily, from the kitchen.

Petatorov pulled a bag of dried rusks and an old steel thermos from behind the cupboard. The thermos was empty. The sweet smell of wine tickled his nostrils, and Petatorov wiped away a tear. He took a bottle from the inside pocket of his overcoat and placed it beside the mattress. It was the only pocket Philip kept an eye on; in it he kept cigarettes, things to eat and, most important of all, bottles and utensils. The pocket was new and good quality, divided into sections, down to the waist in depth, and to the shoulder blades in width. Philip put the kettle on the electric ring, took off his shoes, and leant them against the corner of the stove which protruded from the wall.

He lay down and lit a cigarette. Then he remembered that he had that day brought with him *Venus in Furs*. Never mind, that could wait till tomorrow. He took a glass and with his finger picked at the yellowish-white muck which had dried on the bottom of it. Never mind. He filled the glass, and savoured it for a moment, just like a bridegroom eyeing his naked and nervous bride on his wedding night. Now Phil, in tiny little sips!

Op—op—op

op!

Ah—f—foo—oo!

"Good stuff, this!" thought the lecturer. "*In vino veritas, sed in quanto vino?*"

Ah, now some rusks, soak them in tea and eat them! And this powdered tea is the best in the world.

Petatorov made the tea—strong and bitter. And sugar —two lumps.

I'm lying here, drinking tea—at my leisure. When I have some money, I buy extra bread and make rusks.

It's terrible to depend on your stomach—it drives you to all kinds of mean tricks. At its slightest protest—I give it a rusk, have a rusk, I say! And some tea. And now shut up, you poor old thing.

I don't need anything—oh well, sorry—just a little bottle of wine, anything except vodka. I'm not some common alcoholic—I need wine for my dreams—for my happiness. I don't go to work, I don't give a damn about anything.

Nihilist?

Of course not, I'm already going grey in places, how can I be a nihilist? It's simply that I understand a great deal, so much that I lose heart.

Yes now, that's how I live. I've found the blue bird after all! God, how many of them there are—every bottle has them. Night falls, and the blue bird's mine! "He's gone down-hill!" Well maybe—but what if I'm happy? Who of them can boast he's happy?! He's out of his mind, they say; and they are right because they take happiness to be madness. There, I'll look out of the window at the stars, and then, back to my mattress and I'll pour out another half-glass, and once more, Philip, take it in little tiny sips! Don't hurry! And I'm alone, I'm free, my thoughts race along, here and there, mostly in the past, but whenever it's the future my thoughts bump into, it does not seem radiant at all,[1] the future doesn't, but a fiery Gehenna, which scorches my wings! No thanks, you go on working, all of you, lie, lie, prostitute yourselves to the end, till you get sores on your brains; sometimes you don't even want to prostitute yourselves, but you can't help doing it, because your cowardice and spiritual flabbiness have gone to such extremes; I can see right through you. Sometimes I want to start yelling: come to your senses, while a last tiny

[1] An allusion to the Communist catch-phrase: "Forward to the radiant future!" (*Tr. note*).

spark still smoulders in your heart, what are you thinking of! Say what *you* think, and not what your boss thinks! And I did start yelling once a long time ago, because I couldn't stand it any longer; they almost sacked me, but friends put things right again: they drew up a certificate—that I'd had a fit. And I've got a bad heredity: my grandfather was strung up as an expropriator, and they did something bad to my father, too. But—I'm happy. People say things about me, they pity me, that poor devil Phil. But I sit here, and sense eternity, I, Philip Petatorov, do! What's the use of probing into everything? There isn't anything! God has died! So what, then? I, Petatorov, am my own God, God is in me; no sacrifice, nothing is needed, my Petatorov happiness exists!

Pour me out another little glass, Philip. Drink it down in little tiny sips, little tiny ones, and you get—euphoria. Ha-ha! Now they can't even kill me—the knife melts, and melts, and now it's as soft as a feather. Ah, Petatorov do you remember how you started to disintegrate? You suddenly realized that there was nothing. That you were lying, lying to the point of imbecility, of bestiality; at meetings people pronounced your name wrong: Petatórov! You were livid, but were ashamed to correct them, but once you shouted: not Petatórov, but Petátorov! The speaker apologized and corrected himself: Petátorov. And *I was born*, I, Philip! Oh, there's no freedom: old Gran will throw me out of the flat, and the police will come at once—oh, all that's to do with my body, but my soul is pure, my soul, my diamond! It has broken free, my delicate, my immortal, my only soul! It has broken free! The pig's skin has been torn off my treasure—and here I am, in front of you, in my entirety! "How low he's sunk!" If only you could sink as low! Oh yes, I've lost my standing, ah, and my family, the warmth and the love. "Standing" indeed!

And what if you're lying? Have you regrets, in your heart of hearts?

Petatorov was kneeling in front of the electric ring, watching the kettle.

"Phil, give us a bit of sausage," mumbled the cat in its sleep.

And what if I am lying?

How can one drag truth out of one's innermost heart? The most difficult thing is to own up to oneself, because then one must do something about it.

The tea's good.

Well no, I'm not lying. I may have suspicions—but suspicion purges. Caught you, slave! You've still enough baseness in you to go on living and dreaming!

But no, I'm not vile, not base, my heart's as pure as a leaf in springtime—yes, it is. My coat's torn, my suit's not tip-top, but I'm pure!

. . . Here I am, sitting here, and I'm terrified: I'm alone, face to face with this huge country, with a God who has died. Why are we so unhappy, so indifferent to it all? Why don't we care that we're slaves? God! Why do people live as in a dream: we should run, we should defend ourselves, but our arms and legs are as if made of cotton-wool, and the villains overtake us once more, and break us, and dragoon us. And there's no help for it, because we've been dreamed up by the devil, and that dream is eternal. And I myself, Petatorov, can only run away, and hide, and grieve, and observe with delight how blood falls in drops on the snow, on the mud, on the floor. Blood and grief.

Little tiny sips, Phil, little tiny ones. Don't hurry, there's not much left. And that pain can't be eradicated, Phil, nothing can drown it, beautiful lips cannot kiss it away.

Petatorov wrapped himself up in his coat and a quilted jacket, and sleep gradually overtook him.

And outside it was winter, the usual winter, when everything is covered with snow and the wind blows, when one wants life to stop, and the streets are bathed in the mournful light of swaying lamp-posts, and hardly any people walk the streets and alleys—they will die that night. They are preparing for it, they have no longer any time left and it does not matter whether it is cold or warm. And the wind sprays dry snow on their backs and faces, and sings in a self-satisfied, academic voice: you've got no-o-o-one, no-o-o-one . . . you're alo-o-one . . . soon I'll cover your gra-a-ave with sn-o-o-ow . . . ooooooo . . .

On such a night men anxiously ask the women who are cuddled up to them:

"Do you love me?"

"Yes . . . And you?"

"Yes!"

They are lying on warm beds in warm rooms behind the stone walls of houses, and the houses are in the streets of towns, and countless towns are lost in that vast expanse which is called Russia. Nobody asks Russia about anything, and there she lies, boundless and cold, looking with dead eyes—and not even looking, for her eyes are covered with snow and ashes, they remind one

of the face of a statue from antiquity.[1] Russia is dead,
but men—

Petatorov's dream

Petatorov was freezing as he ran, and met no one.
That evening, unexpectedly, the frost had struck and
paralyzed the town until spring. At the corner he
stumbled against a barrel of beer; a queue of people was
standing motionless. The woman selling the beer had
her hand on the tap, from which protruded a little
column of transparent yellow beer. Her right hand
rested on a pile of coppers. A drunk stood there, frozen
stiff, with a tankard in his hand, others were sitting,
leaning against the round end of the barrel. No steam
issued from their open mouths; one man still had a
herring-tail between his teeth. A woman was dragging
her husband away from the barrel. And they were all
frozen rigid. A policeman with a whistle in his mouth
had raised his truncheon; cars were not moving, only
the traffic-lights were still flashing. An anxious old lady
with a log under her arm had not had time to cross the
street. In a telephone kiosk with its glass broken stood
a man, laughing into the receiver: the wind had piled
up a little snow-drift on his tongue . . . Policemen, beating
a passer-by with their truncheons, had frozen in their
tracks, each in the various steps of the dance of their
official duties.

And no matter how much Philip rushed around, he
could not find a living soul. The snow fell slowly on the

---

[1] It is interesting to compare Turgenev's description of Russia:
". . . that immense dark figure, motionless and veiled, like the sphinx
of Oedipus . . . I seem to see her coarse inert gaze fixed on me with
bleak attention, as befits eyes of stone . . ." (Letter to Pauline
Viardot, 16th May, 1850) (*Tr. note*).

congealed people, they were white and beautiful, and there was no sound of speech.

He ran up Sadovaya Street and saw a column of soldiers. They were marching in step, with great precision. Small detachments went off into the alley-ways. And then began the extermination of the frozen. The soldiers easily chopped up the people who, being icicles, broke with a tinkle. Philip followed the soldiers and saw them fall on Pushkin's statue, and hack and hack at it, till their swords grew blunt, while from the bronze wounds hot red blood flowed, covering the boulevard and the square with ice.

Philip thought he saw figure-skaters hiding in the gateways—another moment, and gay couples would begin to whirl on the skating-rink of blood.

"Idiots! Can't you see that it's a monument!" roared the commanding officer.

"The Egyptians are upon us!" thought Philip.

And the Egyptians were chopping people up, just as if they were ice.

Petatorov was freezing. Tearing away the prickly paws of cold, he was turning to ice, and he saw Nadya, pouring boiling water over him from a kettle, but the water froze up. Petatorov was covered with a thick crust of ice. He forced his mouth open with difficulty, and said:

"Na-dezh-da, rr-u-n . . ."

A soldier came up to him and raised his sword to strike.

"Don't!" Petatorov wanted to shout. "I'm pure and fragile, like ice, ha-ve mer-cy!"—and he heard the crack of his splintering body.

Chapter 2

What to live on?

"Ouf!"

Petatorov was woken by the cold, he was shivering and pulling his unlined coat over his head. Gran had lit the stove, and the logs were jumping and squeaking like rabbits.

"Miaou!" said the cat, pushing the door open with her nose.

"Miaou!" said Petatorov. The cat purred, and squeezed through the door. She came up to the mattress and looked intently at its occupant.

"Well, puss, do you want something to eat?"

"And how!" said the cat.

"Very well, if I manage to get something today—I'll certainly treat you."

The cat waved her tail against her sides in approval.

"Eh, puss, it's cold and there isn't any wine and there's

nothing to eat. Never mind, everything will be all right in the end."

Petatorov got up and put on his coat.

"Oh, let those who can, laugh!"[1] he said, and went to the kitchen.

"Gran, give us a spud."

"There you are—"

"Thanks! I wouldn't mind just one more."

"That's enough! When will you pay me back those 10 roubles?"

"Definitely, very soon. Could I have a cup of tea?"

"Take it, what am I to do with you?"

"Don't grumble, old girl. Give and spend and God will send."

"Go away, go away!"

Petatorov slunk away and out into the street. The door keepers were scattering sand on the ice-covered pavement. A crowd of people stood at the food shop, their heads tilted upwards; bottles, like bugles raised to celebrate a victory, were sticking out of their mouths. Alas! only the gurgle of beer reached Petatorov. They were taking a hair of the dog which had bitten them. His heart sank, he turned away from them and went past with a look of unutterable boredom.

The fog hung in wisps, motionless. A man would go by, and a grey wisp, on the spur of the moment, would make a movement towards him, fail to keep up, and droop sadly again. Petatorov reached the station square, people jostled him, squeezed him, and warmed him up. He went under the bridge and turned into Kalanchevskaya Street. Then through little back alleys, full of dirty tumble-down little houses, he came out into the Meshchanka district. Here, in Sirotski Lane, lived his friend Yuli Sheptunov, who had no definite occupation. Petatorov went into the courtyard, shouted: "Yuli!" and,

[1] A quotation from the poet Khlebnikov (*Tr. note*).

by way of rotten boards at the front door, reached the staircase, and went up to the fifth floor.

The house was like an almshouse: endless corridors, and innumerable doors. It was inhabited by quiet, inconspicuous old ladies: they listened to the radio, mumbled foreign political news to each other, and cooked millet gruel and potatoes. Petatorov went in and heard a conversation coming from the kitchen.

"Yez—Zending a sip into space iz not az eazy az pullink a cat by zee tail . . ."

"Yez, zat's a complicated mazine . . ."

In the depths of the tunnel-like corridor two old ladies were standing, listlessly fighting. One had caught hold of her partner by the sole remaining wisp of hair over her right ear, and was trying to pull it out. The victim was yelping without enthusiasm—not from pain, but just to observe the rules of propriety.

Petatorov and his friend went to the very end of the corridor. At the door of Sheptunov's room stood a large packing case in which a television set had been delivered; in this Yuli kept potatoes. The room was the breadth of three men, and the length of two lying down head to toes. Immediately by the entrance came one end of a narrow bed; by the window stood a table and chair, and a record-player. On the walls—a collection of suns: golden, red, blue, green, cheerful and sad suns; they seemed to light up the room. Over the door—shelves with books.

"Want some tea, Philip?"

"I wouldn't say no!"

Yuli went out to the kitchen, while Petatorov lay down on the bed. He felt warm and comfortable: he was at his friend's, he was about to have some tea and talk to Yuli; one could talk about everything with him. Yuli understood everything, and there was nothing to fear from him. Can one really trust anyone in this world?

Yes, oh yes, and that's why the world has not yet fallen to pieces. People clung to each other, hanging on the frail thread of trust—over an abyss. Sometimes one, sometimes another falls into it, having lost all hope of *starting to live*; and those people are pushed from behind by a crowd of their fellow citizens; in uniform and out of it, good and evil, and all sorts of others . . .

"Here, take the glass, Philip. By the way, how are you off for money?"

"Haven't any."

"Things are a bit tight with me, too, but yesterday I sold a good book for just as good money, here's three roubles."

"Thanks. You're kind to me, Yuli. I can't earn anything myself any more. The malevolence of men has worn me out. How unlucky we've been, Yuli! We've landed in hell, and we're alive! You're ten years younger than me, and perhaps you can see a way out. But I am poisoned. I don't see any means of stopping people— they are going to Lucifer's feast and snatch bits from each other so as to arrive at his table well-fed! There's no God, He has died, and instead of Him in people's hearts there's the Politgramota."[1]

"Yet all the same, Philip, kindness slumbers in them, and it will awake . . . I'm convinced of it."

"Ha-ha! Their kindness goes no further than giving up a seat in a bus to an old woman. Potential kindness, and reigning evil! Why should the former awaken? The evil spirit is too resourceful, every toady is a worker for it. What is God? A frame of mind—goodness; and what is a brute?—also a frame of mind. There's nothing to be done if there's a brute lodged inside you, you can't smoke him out! No, Yuli. People will play themselves

[1] *Politgramota*: A collection of doctrinal political clichés, setting out the basic principles of Soviet communism, taught in Soviet educational establishments (*Tr. note*).

out unto death, till nothing is left of them. The frail strings will snap and—it is the end, death. Personally, I've escaped in time. However, it is, perhaps, just at that point that the wild beast will be purified by death and blood, and become a human being? And again: who will be victorious this time: God, or the brute? And the most terrible thing, Yuli, which makes me suffer as I do, is that I don't believe there will be a *this time* . . ."

"Philip, your tea's getting cold."

"Yes, yes."

Petatorov took the mug and lay back again. He was tense and nervous.

"Philip, did you come to me for comfort?"

"Yes! Help me. Tell me what you think. Tell me, Yuli. I'm thirty-six and I'm already sick to death of everything. They killed my father, just like that, for no reason—took him away and killed him. I did my studies and, instead of philology, I studied the works of the Seminarist.[1] Oh, Lord! And then—it was a nightmare: tyranny didn't die with the tyrant; tyranny is versatile and cunning, it's eternal, because it has taken up its abode within men . . ."

"Philip, I'll tell you a parable. In spite of all your learning, you don't know it . . ."

The Parable of the Chest

It came to pass that some people found themselves living in a dark box—a chest of ancient workmanship—through which light could not penetrate. They could stand up and even walk about in it, and that was all. An Evil Spirit jumped and capered on the lid; the people

[1] i.e. Stalin (*Tr. note*).

still remembered what the light of day was like, and they wanted to get out into the world—and live! They bore children, grew old and died. The children grew up with little green faces and weak heads; the lack of air and sunshine gave most of them rickets and soft, deformed skulls. They, too, bore children, planted potatoes and—grew old and, quietly and with dignity, went off to the next world. One day, they discovered in a corner of the chest a very old man, who whispered: "I am dying . . . I used to know a great deal, and even remember a time when I was not sitting in the chest! It was wonderful! And all my life in the pitch dark I've been writing a treatise: 'How to get out of the chest.'" And the old man gave up the ghost. The green faces were unable to read the treatise, since it was as dark as ever. From time to time they could hear someone knocking outside; some people were delighted, and said: "Oh, they are repairing the chest! They're probably putting iron bands round it! How splendid! We can live peacefully, and carry on planting potatoes." Others were sorry, but did not show it; secretly, when the others were asleep, they would climb up to the ceiling, trying to open the lid, but the Evil Spirit was jumping and dancing on top of it. And suddenly a misfortune befell the Evil Spirit: the ring of the padlock rusted and the padlock fell off! The green faces trembled at the terrible crash, but the most daring and inquisitive amongst them climbed up to the ceiling, and half-opened the lid. Wind and sunshine burst into the chest! The stream of fresh air made many of the green faces feel ill, and they burst into tears, thinking they were dying. On realizing what had happened the Evil Spirit jumped on the lid, and stuck carrots and cabbage-stumps into the fastenings to hold them; but inquisitive people were pushing from below! And to this very day the Evil Spirit is still unable to bang the lid shut; sometimes the flap of a coat sticks over the edge, sometimes the green faces put a hand out, or a head—and heads roll. The green faces have woken up, and now they're afraid: "what if they suddenly bang it shut?! We shall suffocate!"

And in the glimmering light on the floor of the chest other green faces are reading the old grey-beard's treatise: "How to get out of the chest." And the rest of the green faces slowly begin to feel themselves human and, although it frightens them, they can guess by now at the delights of daylight and fresh air.

Pale-faced, Petatorov was lying on his bed and looking at the hundreds of suns hanging on the wall.

"It's a good parable," he said.

Yuli poured out the remains of the tea.

"Do you think they will no longer put heads under lids?"

Yuli shrugged his shoulders.

"Yuli," Petatorov whispered, "help me to believe it . . ."

Sheptunov had a pang of anguish as he looked at Philip—at his sallow face, torn coat, bit of blanket instead of a scarf.

Nothing would help him . . . nothing . . . tram-ta-ra-ram!

"Yuli," Philip jumped up and leaned over Sheptunov. "Yuli," he said in a whisper, "do you know what the last line of the treatise is?" Petatorov giggled. "In order to get out of the chest, one must first see the light of day."

Sheptunov gave a start, struck by the conviction in Philip's voice.

"What faith have you in *misfortune*!"

"I have, I have," cried Petatorov. "This is the only

thing I encounter every day, every hour! It is not a legend or a dream. Not once have I told a stranger what I think—even about football! I lied to my students, and then I used to go home and drink, so as to forget their trusting faces! And later I understood: they knew I was lying and could do nothing but lie! That *such was my work*! I was selling my soul for consumption on and off the premises! I would take my pen—and it would automatically write lying words! And no one believed them, because they were printed in Russia and their author was not in prison."

Petatorov was worn out. He was shaking, sweat was dripping from his forehead.

Sheptunov looked stonily at Van Gogh's sun.

"You haven't been through that, Yuli. You're an innocent pauper—but I—I've been raped—depraved. They came and asked me: Oh, you're not a party member yet? And I hummed and hawed: No, I need more ground-work, need more . . . And they asked me gently: what do you want? To work on Latin authors here, or to teach arithmetic in Bugul'ma?[1] They knew, they've got a well-tried method, they knew I was just a common whore."

Sheptunov stirred a little.

"Philip, but now everything's all right, you're free, you wouldn't lie to me, would you?"

"I don't know. I've got nothing left. I'm like an insane old man amid the smoking ruins of his home. I might find a saucepan, or my little grand-daughter's ribbon, and cry for joy. I've got nothing to stake on a card—I'm a pauper. What did I snatch from the jaws of Moloch? All I have left is you and my landlady's cat."

Sheptunov turned to the record player and put on a record of organ music.

[1] Remote provincial town (*Tr. note*).

"Yuli, is there any tea left?" asked Petatorov; he looked dejected and grey.

Sheptunov took the kettle and went out.

"I'll run off somewhere. I need cold and poverty in order to have no memory of anything! I must forget everything, I think too much. I have two huge worries—bread and wine. And I'll read something . . .

Bread.

Wine.

Ten roubles for my landlady.

A bit of sausage for puss.

Petatorov was listening to Bach and he was beginning to feel calmer and better. Oh, my unhappy brothers! We're dispersed through every country and all ages, and we shall stretch out our hands to each other, and support the weak and the stumbling, we're strong because Bach is one of us, and so is melancholy Franz. Our grief is great, and a word or a sound will make the cup overflow, and out will gush a torrent of moans, treacheries, love and sorrow, and men will be struck with horror and men will see themselves in their true light.

This is what we shall do, my unhappy brothers! Who, but us, grieves over man unrealized, who but us damns the self-satisfied slave?

"Yuli," said Petatorov to Sheptunov as he came in, "I'll go and have dinner with my sister, I haven't been there for a month."

"Why don't you stay? There's a potato and half a herring, we'll cook them and clean them and eat them."

"Oh Yuli, why waste so much of everything on me when I can eat with my family?"

They left the room, and followed the narrow tunnel to the way out.

The two old ladies had stopped fighting and were chatting in a corner.

"That'z juzt vat I zay: their rocketz fly vorze than ourz do."

"Yez . . . Vhy, zey zaid on the radio: ze launching haz been pozponed again, becauze of muddle . . ."

"But ourz—vork properly. Poof!—and they're there, poof! and they've taken a znap of the moon . . ."

"Yez."

"Drop in again, Philip," said Sheptunov. "I'll find you a little job—something easy."

"Thanks, Yuli. I will."

"Oh Philip," thought Sheptunov. "How bitter you are. They've crushed you and trampled on you. You are not fit to live. And the sooner you die, the better. If only a woman could grow fond of you, you'd revive a bit, but then you'd torture her with pure, merciless words, crush her with analysis. And you would die too, tormented by the thought that you had destroyed her for no reason. However, he is quite aware himself that no one would agree to bear his pain for him."

And Sheptunov thought of how it would be if Petatorov were dead. He was filled with sorrow and loneliness gripped him, and a sweet lump rose in his throat.

stop Yuli you're burying Phil too soon stop

Sheptunov went back to his room. Today he was going to have an important meeting with Comrade Shulyatko. He pulled a suitcase from under the bed. There . . . a bundle of magazines . . . and he also asked for a book.

D. H. Lawrence. Hm, Shulyatko can't even read Russian properly . . . Very well, I'll keep it down to six magazines and some postcards.

· ·

Eh! There's a really hard frost today. And the pavements are covered with ice. Oh!

Sheptunov took the metro to the centre of the city. Not far from the metro station stood a large gloomy building covered with memorial plaques. Here lived Comrade Shulyatko. His position in the hierarchy was such that Yuli was afraid to name it even to himself. One felt less uneasy if one didn't know it. I don't know —and that's that. And thank God I don't.

And Sheptunov crossed the threshold. A figure draped in furnishing material detached itself from the wall.

"Where are you going?" asked the figure.

"Flat 37."

The draped figure took out a paper and checked the time.

"Surname?"

"Sheptunov."

"Other names?"

"Yuli Adamovich."

"Year of birth?"

"1940."

"Go in."

Sheptunov went up to the second floor and rang a bell. The door was opened by a beautiful, muscular girl.

"Would you please tell Comrade Shulyatko that Yuli is here?"

"Just a moment," the beautiful girl replied with a

strong French accent. A draught made the door swing, clanking on a chain. Not for the first time Yuli was struck by this chain—it was of magnificent workmanship, obviously handmade. The girl came back and took off the chain . . . She led Sheptunov into a little room; the furniture—just a table and two small chairs. No windows. In the wall—a small door, like the one which Buratino[1] opened with a little golden key. The door from the corridor opened, and in came Comrade Shulyatko—balding, stately, no wrinkles, small, reddish eyes. In pyjamas and slippers.

"What have you brought?"

"Six magazines and some photographs."

"How much?"

"Ten roubles each."

"Fifty."

"Seventy."

"I could get all these magazines free."

"I know," said Sheptunov slowly. "But I also know that it's better for you to get them from me for money."

"Show your goods."

Yuli undid his magazines. Shulyatko's eyes sparkled.

"Hm! That's the stuff."

And with studied carelessness Shulyatko examined the photographs of naked women in various Yoga gymnastic poses. He did not even notice how his hand took out his wallet and unerringly counted out seven red banknotes.

"Do you still need me?"

"What? . . . said Shulyatko. He had taken a magnifying glass and, pink and excited, was examining the vital spot on the photo.

"Wait!" he said suddenly and began speaking abruptly "I need a reliable man for half an hour once a fortnight."

---

[1] Buratino—character in A. N. Tolstoy's fairy-tale, based on the Italian *Pinocchio* (*Tr. note*).

"A homosexual?" asked Sheptunov quickly.

"No!" said Shulyatko with a frown. "You're always so filthy-minded! He wouldn't have to do anything like that, he'd only have to walk around my room in there (he pointed to the little door in the wall) holding . . . well, let's say . . . mm—some metal object . . . in his hand . . ."

Sheptunov went over a dozen perversions in his memory. Nothing appropriate.

"All right," said Yuli. "I'll do my best. So, a hundred for him, and ten for me as the go-between. And my man won't suffer any harm?"

"Of course not! But he must be reliable, must be trusted not to gossip anywhere. If he gossips, I'll put him inside, and you too. Get out."

"Good-bye, Comrade Shulyatko."

"Toulousa!" called the boss, "show Yuli out."

The silent, muscular girl closed the door behind Sheptunov. The chain rattled.

In the hall the same man was on duty.

"Halt!" he said. "Where from?"

"From No. 37."

"Surname?"

"Sheptunov."

"Other names?"

"Yuli Adamovich."

"Year of birth?"

"1940."

The man took out some photos and compared them with Yuli.

"Came in at 11.00?"

"Yes."

The figure leant towards the wall.

"Petya, No. 966 is leaving. Identical with the photos. How about you?"

"All right," the wall whispered. "Let him go."

Sheptunov opened the door and went out. He wiped the sweat from his forehead.

Well, there's a nice little job for Petatorov, and not so dusty, either. A hundred roubles for half an hour! He'll be able to take a nice room with a woman, smarten himself up . . .

. . . .

The old man threw some pine extract cubes into the bath. The doctor had told him to take a medicinal bath for ten minutes twice a month. And for five whole months. He tried the water—it was too hot. Ah, yes, to-day he had bought an hour-glass, so as not to stay in too long. The old man shuffled into the next room and took a package from the windowsill. He looked out of the window. It was cold out there. The building opposite looked dead, with curtains covering its eye-sockets. The old man saw someone come out of the entrance, stand still for a moment, and then go off somewhere. "That's strange. Some ragamuffin or other." He looked at the house again—a nasty chill of terror crawled in his stomach. If only someone would look out! It was just as if the blind and the dead had taken up residence there! The old man went back to the bathroom and dipped his fingers in the green water. There was a smell of pine planks. Yes, now it was all right. He took off his pyjama top, under-pants and shirt, moved a stool close to his bath, and carefully—so as not to slip—lowered his shrivelled, useless body into the hot water. Aaaai, lovely! The warmth flowed over his joints; the old man gently turned over the hour glass.

Chapter 3

Dinner with the Family

Petatorov was running along the icy street.

What are these people interested in? Wake up! Drummers, beat the alarm! Crawl out of your holes! Fight! Sound the alarm, sound the alarm.

Before it's too late!

Sound the alarm! Don't hand over the bugle to the Archangel—he'll play a different tune.

Oh?!

"You shouldn't run in front of an oncoming car like that," said the policeman gently.

"No, indeed not," said Petatorov, startled, and sup-

pressed a desire to go down on his knees. And he murmured like a prayer Vladimir Solovyov's lines:

> I shall not cause a breach of the peace,
> But you must have compassion;
> You must not torment my soul,
> But let me go in peace!

"That's all right, off you go."

His sister lived at the other end of town. Petatorov
took a bus and went there.

Would she be glad to see her brother? What difference
does it make? She'll feed me, won't throw me out—she'd
be ashamed to, because of the neighbours. Ha ha! But
she doesn't like it: a senior lecturer, has published
learned papers, is respected—and then suddenly he goes
off his rocker. A family disgrace!

Ha-ha! Ha!

I haven't *disgraced* you much yet! I was senior lecturer, ha! ha! Came up from nothing and became a
senior lecturer.

I wouldn't mind something to eat. She'll probably
give me a little drink. She and her husband don't drink,
but on festive occasions it's all according to the book.
"Everything must be just like other people." Oh, my
progressive sister! Chairman of the House Sprites' Com-
mittee.[1] Oh, my ideologically steadfast sister! When I
left everything—she came to see me. "Aren't you
ashamed of yourself, Philip?" I laughed in her face and
said calmly: "Go away, my dear, I'll wring your neck."
And the dear went.

Then she resigned herself to it— after all, I am her

---

[1] A play on words, which purposely confuses the house committees
which exist in Soviet blocks of flats with house sprites or hob-
goblins (*Tr. note*).

brother. She sent a letter through Nadya. "Come," she said.

The bus rumbled over the ruts and bumps of the road. And past it went little tiny boxes, bigger boxes, big boxes, divided into compartments for people. Go on living, my dear people.

How grey and boring! Someone (Goethe?) said: architecture is frozen politics. From the silly shiny buns on top of steeples—to the little tiny boxes . . .

"It's the terminus!" shouted the driver. "Hey, you there!"

"Hey, you there." He means me. And what about me? I shan't cause a breach of the peace . . .

"Hello, my dear Larisa, how glad I am to see you!" declaimed Petatorov pompously.

"Hello."

Petatorov discarded his coat— and went to the kitchen.

"Hello, soup, how glad I am to smell you!"

"We're just going to eat, wash your hands, Philip, and then go into the sitting-room."

"Uncle Philip's come," his nephew rejoiced.

"Hello, nephew! Are you just as much of a dolt as you always were?"

His nephew scowled.

"Hello, lawful wedded husband of my dear sister! Are you just as . . ."

"Stop it, Philip!" Alexey Semyonovich, Larisa's husband and head of a department, cut him short. And he went away into the kitchen. There they began whispering, then talking loudly.

Petatorov listened to the quarrel with glee.

"He . . . he's the fifth column in our family!" shouted Alexey Semyonovich. "He's flouted the most sacred, not to mention the elementary standards of behaviour! He should be in a lunatic asylum! He should be expelled from the hero-city.[1] Lousy polyglot! Sponger!"

"Don't, Alexey darling, he's so unhappy, after all he's quite alone, you know, he's ill . . . Don't make a scene, please don't. He comes to see us once a year, have a little patience . . ."

"He corrupts our son! Look how pleased the boy is to see him, for six months he's been saying nothing but Uncle! Uncle!"

Petatorov warmed to the boy a bit.

"Nephew," he said. "Don't be cross. I'm not just an ordinary uncle, I'm your mad uncle. Come and talk to me. I believe you're just finishing school?"

His nephew beamed.

"Yes, Uncle Philip. I'm going to be a philologist—like you."

Philip was embarrassed.

"Oh, my dear nephew, you want to go mad too!?"

"No, Uncle, you're not mad, you're noble."

"Yes, I'm a noble madman . . ."

His sister brought in a steaming saucepan.

"Oh, at last! My dear sister, how that saucepan does suit you!"

Alexey Semyonovich was silent. Larisa was carving the meat.

"Sis," said Petatorov gently, "I suppose you wouldn't have any . . . you know, what's it . . ."

Larisa got up in silence and went to the sideboard.

[1] Moscow was given the title "Hero-city" at the end of the war in 1945 (*Tr. note*).

"Thanks, Lara. You're kind, and I'm horrid."
And he drank a glass of port.
They were all silent.
"They've sent us a new director now," said Alexey Semyonovich morosely. "A Jew."
"Well, and so what?" asked Petatorov.
"Nothing. He's a Jew."

. . . .

Beer and Sheptunov. Still life: Sheptunov with beer. Half a glass of beer—a gulp of cold apple juice. Enough. He got up—reeled—left.

Hop-hop home! I only hope I won't meet a . . . centurion. Steady, Sheptunov.
Must help Philip.
Shall I go to his wife, and tell her? How long since they saw each other? Many years, yes, yes. They've forgotten each other.
But I go on reading. I go on and on reading. And how clever you've become, Yuli Adamovich.
I must go to Petatorov's placc. A hundred roubles for half an hour!
Hop-hop!

He opened the door of his room and fell on the bed.

I'll go this evening; he's sure to be loafing around a food shop. I'll wai . . .

. . . .

"Well, and so what?!" shouted Philip.

"Nothing. You can't throw a stone without hitting a Jew, they're everywhere."

"Ha! Ha! If there weren't any, you'd die of boredom. Why, that's a splendid subject! Somewhere to throw a stone and feel a certain superiority—look, I too can do something! You can set your head in action—or rather, not head, but just pressed straw!"

"Philip!" said his sister warningly.

"You don't know them!" Alexey Semyonovich was now shouting too.

"Little by little, and using all their guile, they're pushing out us Russians. They think we're fools! Us Russians—FOOLS!"

"In my opinion that was established ages ago," said Petatorov calmly. "There's no reason to doubt it."

Alexey Semyonovich gave a start.

"There you are, Larochka, that's your brother in one for you. But I was told only yesterday what they do to our children! They turn them into idiots!"

"What do you mean?"

"When children are vaccinated at school, they don't allow their children to be done, because the vaccine is specially poisoned, so that the Russian children will grow up to be fools. Then it'll be easier for them to worm their way in."

"Alexey, the Jews must have bathed you in that vaccine, you've become so . . ."

"Philip!" his sister cut him short. "Stop it, both of you, talk about something else."

"But there's nothing else to talk about, is there, Alexey?"

Silence reigned.

"So you want to be a philologist? Then I believe you must speak English rather well, dear nephew?"

"Yes, Uncle Philip."[1]

And they isolated themselves from his parents by means of incomprehensible words. Alexey Semyonovich, shocked, was nevertheless in his heart of hearts proud of his son's knowledge.

"Nephew, it's possible that I won't come to see you again for some time. Think over what I am going to say to you. Politics have occupied so much space in this country that everything has become dominated by them —everything that's expressed in words and not in mathematical signs. Mathematics are not dangerous to officials, on the contrary, mathematics will create new weapons and little devices for listening and spying. But words are dangerous, they can shout about goodness and love! Do you understand me, nephew?"

"Yes!"

"To be or not to be . . . it sounds nonsense nowadays! I would say: to lie or not to lie, to be crazy or to betray . . ."[1]

"Stop corrupting the child," said Alexey Semyonovich who hadn't understood a word, but was bursting with esteem for the university professor.

There was silence.

Larisa was clearing the table.

"I'll help you," said Petatorov, and took the plates to the kitchen.

---

[1] In English in the original (*Tr. note*).

Chapter 4

In the Editorial Offices of an Important Newspaper

Messengers are running. Typewriters are tapping. Proofs are being corrected. Paper. Type. Ink. They're printing. Loading. Dispatching. Hands put down a coin and take a paper. People read it. They wrap a sandwich up in it. They spread it on a dirty bench—so as to sit on it and kiss someone. They take it to the lavatory.

Read it. Take out a subscription. Three hundred and sixty-five days in the year the paper mice rustle and with their little paws swiftly, pleasantly, rub the modest little spot where brains ought to be.

Vasili Velzin is a progressive journalist. He understands a great many things, but does not always write about them in the paper. He has written about a lot of things on toilet paper. If all the columns written by Vasili Velzin were to be stretched out end to end, you could use it two hundred times.

. . . .

Petatorov looked at his sister. She had aged and was tired. She was washing up in a mechanical way. My dear sister! Why had that chap treated her like that?! Ah, the swine!

"Larochka!"

"Yes?"

"Forgive me. I'm sorry. I won't come to you again. I've tormented all of you. I'm ill, Larochka. I can't do anything about myself. I envy people: why do they feel all right—or tolerably well! Why aren't they in shreds like me?! Forgive me, Larochka!"

Hysterically, he was pulling his coat off the hanger.

"Philip!"

"Ah Larochka, I'm finished, finished, finished."

Petatorov was running along the street—running away!

But someone ran out from a doorway after him!

Away!

Must wear myself out with running.

Afraid of looking round, Phil?

It's Professor P. A. Petatorov, trotting after you!

"Philip!" A woman's voice called despairingly.

Like someone calling "Help!"

He came to.

A huge grey building,—inside the building there's rustling, rustling, just as if it were filled to the roof with mice.

There's someone I know here.

"Comrade Velzin is busy," said the secretary, showing her sharp little teeth. "Comrade Velzin is seeing (her voice became a squeak) Kirill Pafnutyevich Sablezubov-Sorbonnov.[1] It's a very important meeting. Come back in half an hour."

[1] Sabretooth—Sorbonne (*Tr. note*).

Petatorov looked with regret at the door, twice as tall as a man, and upholstered with mammoth skin.

"Comrade Velzin, please only edit the style of the article. For tomorrow's issue. There's only two weeks left before the holidays."

Velzin looked through the article. Sablezubov re-read it over Velzin's shoulder. He was still burning with creative fire, and the parting with his brain child was painful to him.

"What rot," thought Velzin, from habit putting in missing commas. "It's all been discussed and rediscussed —and here it is again."

"When finally," Sablezubov was thinking, "we 上用 with all these people. They think what they like! They've lost all sense of discipline! The decisions of our 斗争 must be applied in practice 坚决. When everyone is imbued with 坚急进，上，又不是全 for imperialism, 异化价们工尺管个 for rotten art! No! We will not allow our 工件尺管复命，么, to be slandered 心急无里了. Self-criticism and 下众个坚努山堂 —that's our weapon. Fighting for purity 无尺有急之净本 of our ranks, 文铭尺尸所 survivals, we are going forward to the victory of 的革命.

When 尼征属, because 能的无尸阶级的具理，足为代复展别最高水平的马克思 we 口人民的胜一的什, they 毛泽东思想足革命的科学，足经过长期革命斗争管全党全军 列宁主义，足系统完整的马克思列 utterly 铜锡。我们反对中国主义，反对凡!!!"

"兹叙同死同山一九六〇—六二个星期的总争地发展党发展此会主义的四复大参馆！"[1]

Velzin corrected a spelling-mistake and rang. "Mousey," he said to the secretary who came in, "take this article to be printed. Take out that humorous story. Comrade Sablezubov-Sorbonnov's article is to go in."

Sablezubov put on his hat and took his leave.

In the doorway he bumped into someone looking like

[1] Fragments of Chinese political slogans cut up at random (*Tr. note*).

a tramp, who let him pass. "Who the hell is this queer bird—代伊正立义和岳闩瓦!" thought Sablezubov.

"Hullo, Vasya!" said Petatorov.

"Phil! You're as unexpected as a pistol shot!"

They embraced and sat down, chuckling as they lit their cigarettes. "Vasya, you're in good form and cheerful! How do you do it?"

"And you're mocking, as always; but gloomy."

"Yes, yes. I'm tired, Vasya, and I'm looking for work."

"But Philip, aren't you a senior lecturer! Have you left the institute?"

"Long ago. Now I'm NOBODY."

"No money?"

"None. I worked in the summer, unloading vans. But now—it doesn't matter . . ."

But what about Nadya, Phil?"

"I left her."

"What happened?"

"The toady is dead. Long live the madman! I'm as free as a bird. Consequently—I'm a pauper. Vasili Velzin, it's amazing! I read my favourite books and drink port. I am sailing on an ice-flow, shouting to the people left behind: Greetings, rats and mice! Ha! Ha! And you're one of them too. Oh, Lord! Stop soiling lavatory paper with words, give it back to the people—clean! Come on, let's go away together!"

"And live on what?"

"We'll see."

"That's not possible, Philip. I'm here at my post. What you are saying is the apologia of uselessness. If I leave, who will help people, be it ever so little?"

"Really! You've actually found people?"

"Yes! They have a hard life, they're unsettled and unhappy."

"Oh youthful Diogenes! Let them stay like that—they do not tell lies, and only worry about their bread and butter. Or do you want them to pay for it all in the same way that I'm paying?"

"Ah!" Velzin sighed. "We all want changes and are slowly moving towards concessions. Little by little . . ."

"That is copy-book rubbish, my dear Diogenes. Shameless people hire even more shameless people as their assistants. The former even have a slight advantage—they believe in it all just a little. Shamelessness has become our tradition. We believe in neither God, nor Russia, nor ourselves. We're decomposing, Vasya . . ."

The secretary came in.

"Sign here, Comrade Velzin: they've issued us with two mouse traps and 18 pounds of rat poison."

Velzin scribbled something.

"We no longer dream of heaven, Diogenes Velzin. We don't dream of finding a man. We no longer dream at all. It's terrifying to dream nowadays, after all, dreams are realized . . ."

"Philip," said Velzin. "One must work in order to live."

"One mustn't."

"You scrape up a living, by means of windfalls—I can't do that."

"I sometimes steal bottles!" said Petatorov, embarrassed.

"There, you see!" said Velzin, delighted.

"*Quod licet Jovi non licet bovi.*"

"Meaning, translated . . .?"

"Roughly: each man according to his rank."

"Indeed! Each man values nothing but his own. Nothing links us together any more. Men are solitary—they run along the street in order to hide in their holes and sit by their lonely selves. And they drink—like you. There was a lot of talk in Russia about brotherhood; but it turned out that you needed a crowd to shout to a tyrant: tyranize, my dear fellow! But now, it's boring. Petty scoundrels don't know how to hypnotize people. They're ridiculous. Phil, everything must be saved!"

"But we laugh when we're together, and then we separate to weep alone. Men had a God, and He was chopped up on the executioner's block, everyone got a little bit; a quarter of an ear, a bit of finger nail or a slice of heart. We're dispersed, while remaining together. That's why they hate the Jews; they've been dispersed for thousands of years and have remained brothers. Suffering hasn't killed long-suffering."

"Well, what's to be done?"

"Let's go."

"And leave everything to the scoundrels?"

"Yes! They use you to create an illusion of understanding and good will. Deprive them of yourself! Let the red, insolently naked face of the brute appear to the world!"

"It seems to me that prisoners are not indifferent to the sort of warder they have. They're better off if he's kind."

"Give prisoners the keys! Let them escape!"

"I have no keys . . ."

"Ha! Ha! And you, a kind man, whisper words of comfort, through the key-hole! But they are condemned for life. And when they see your kind eye in the peep-hole—they feel better. You walk along the corridor—as kind as kind—and you want to reach the staircase and go out—the door to it is locked, and you see just as kind an eye looking at you—that's your warder, and he's a prisoner too! Escape, Diogenes Velzin. Before the mice have nibbled off your ears. Before you think: Lord, after all, they're right!"

"I must stay."

"Well, then—farewell, Vasya."

"See you soon, fugitive."

And Petatorov left.

Velzin sighed and looked for a long time at the grey window: dirt, cold, and boredom. He opened the drawer of the table and took out an album full of matchbox labels. A flicker of joy crossed the progressive journalist's tired, kind face, as he stroked the labels: red, violet, yellow—as if autumn leaves had fallen straight into the album. He felt happy and forgot about Petatorov. There were the early Russian ones—expensive, rare. And this one—unique in the whole of Eurasia; he'd been offered 10 roubles for it, and refused. His little labels would never let him down, unlike friends and women, they belonged to him—for ever. To him alone! They could be caressed, stroked. And this one with the combine harvester on it—no one else had it; pleasant thought— that. Governments could change, but the labels were unchanging and eternal, like . . . God.

Velzin forgot that working hours were over and that he could go home—oh, it was so nice here, it was only now that life was beginning; he could finger the labels and prepare for ecstasy. Just him—and his little labels . . .

Something clicked and squeaked in the corner. Velzin gave a start and looked in that direction.

A mouse had been caught in the mousetrap . . . Poor thing . . .

He tore himself away from the album and went to the window. The mouse was already growing cold, crushed by the coarse spring. Velzin freed the victim and thought- fully stroked its dense fur.

"You've been caught all right! One . . . two . . . three . . . four little paws . . . and a little tail."

Velzin threw the mouse out of the window and went back to the table.

Thousands of subtle distinctions! Not everyone could master them—a small defect—and the value went up, you must keep your eyes skinned. Velzin's gaze wandered over the walls—and they ceased to exist . . .

The secretary glanced into the office and saw Velzin bent over the album. She sighed with bitterness and prepared to go home. The journalist would sit there till morning, resticking and sorting the labels, and no power could drag him **away.**

. . . In the snack bar on the floor below, Petatorov drank some beer. He bought some sausage for the cat.

In the cloakroom a mouse ran past him, squeaking; a huge fluffy tom was chasing after it.

Home!

Aha! Someone had forgotten a bottle on the windowsill. With an easy gesture he put it in his roomy pocket.

I'm getting weaker.

Must get a bus home—but I want to lie down.

Must get there.

how low he's sunk

     he's *mad*

      HOW LOW HE'S SUNK

        VERY LOW INDEED

That's about me, Phil Petatorov. Does it hurt me? Am I frightened?

Petatorov was walking home a round about way. He was afraid of brightly-lit streets.

Over there, crowds of people with grave faces—coming to meet me, the arch-buffoon. And they shout:

"How low he's sunk!"

"He's mad!"

But I'll take the back ways, I'll creep in and lock the door after me.

He was in a hurry, for a long time he couldn't lock the door.

The cat jumped off the chair and ran up to him, purring.

"Puss, I've brought you some sausage."

The cat opened its eyes wide.

Petatorov shook out the contents of his pocket. Good heavens, as well as the sausage—a bottle of port, a tin of fish in tomato sauce, six hard-boiled eggs, a piece of cheese, and a carefully wrapped buckling—oh, what an aroma of the solid life!

My darling sister had had time to put all this . . .

A drink—quick!

"Phil, how tasty this 2 roubles 90 sausage is!" murmured the cat, with its mouth full.

I'm alone. I'm weak, it's all no use, I can't do anything any more. They've all gone away.

Little tiny sips, Phil.

Hey! Someone! Take away this pain, help me! I haven't done any harm to anyone, have I? So why attack me? Oh Lord! Help me!

Nadya! Where are you?

Aaaah! I'm not a Prague cake! Take your knives away!

And wine doesn't help, nothing helps, o-o-o-h!

Petatorov's hands were tearing up the bedding, he was tense all over.

And then he saw her: Nadya noiselessly entered the room.

"Nadya, darling! Help me!"

She smiled wryly.

Oh, what a lot of guests: Lara, Sheptunov, Velzin and I don't know who those are—I've forgotten.

"Philip!" said Nadya in ringing tones. "Get up! We're going to have fun!"

Philip went up to his guests.

"How did you find out where I live?"

"We know everything!" said the guests in a chorus. "Let's have fun, let's laugh!"

"Get in a circle!" Velzin ordered, and he seized Philip by the hand. And the circle began to turn! The torches flared up—so, so brightly! Confetti showered down, a paper streamer flew up, the guests began to sing in muted tones:

> "We have not come here to booze
> But our Philip to amuse
> To attenuate his pain
> Let us laugh and laugh again!
> Let us shout in merry chorus:
> Do be happy, Petatórov!"

> "Not Petatórov, but Petátorov!"

> Philip longs for joy to start—
> For ages he's been sick at heart;
> So cheer up, dear Philip, do,
> We have brought a bride for you.

> Let us shout in merry chorus
> Do be happy Petatórov!"

"Petátorov!"

"Then you wouldn't scan," said the guests, and sniggered. They began to dance faster. Someone shrouded in white entered the ring. They were now singing in a solemn whisper:

> "Let us question now the bride:
> Who should lie down by her side?
> And to whom is promised bliss?
> Hers the choice! That man or this?
> Any man would jubilate
> But most of all—our candidate!"[1]

"I want Petatorov!" the white-clad figure said in a thin voice.

Everyone vanished. Petatorov pulled off the veil covering the face.

Sheptunov stood facing him.

"You, Yuli?!"

"Ha Ha!" Sheptunov laughed shrilly, and with his long, gloved hand he threw off his mask. The plaster was shattered, a painted eye rolled towards Petatorov's feet.

"Nadezhda!!"

Philip laughed, and he was happy. He put his arms round her and kissed her. Her lips were frozen plums.

"Hah ha!" Nadezhda screeched, and passed her hand across the back of her head: her mask fell off. Petatorov froze—before him, with grinning mouth, stood Death.

"No-o-o-o!"

He seized her by the skull and tried to find the ribbon

[1] Pun on the Russian for the equivalent to a doctor (of philosophy, etc) *candidate of sciences* (*Tr. note*).

at the back of her head, he scratched her temples to pull off the mask.

"Don't, Philip. It's not a mask," said Death. "I am yours, darling."

Petatorov pressed his hands against his bride's ribs, and tried to push her away from him, but Death bent over him groping for his lips . . .

"Miaouaouaou!"

Petatorov was sitting in a corner, shaking. The cat was waving its tail and looking tenderly at Philip.

Where is she?!
Gone—for long?
No, no, I'll lock myself in and I won't go anywhere. I must sleep. I am afraid here. Nowhere to hide.

Petatorov was drinking the wine straight from the bottle, shaking.

He crawled up to his bedding.

You must go to sleep, Phil. You'll go mad. Stop thinking, Phil.

Tired out by his visitors, Petatorov dozed off.

. . . .

Sheptunov woke up. There was rustling behind the door.

"No, don't take zat bat one!"

The old women were stealing potatoes again. Must think up something to stop them, but what?

Sheptunov banged the door with his fist and thundered:

"I can hear you, you old witches!"

He heard the crash of a bucket and the dull thud of falling tubers. There were footsteps running down the corridor, like wind rustling leaves.

Oh!

He got up, pulled a trunk out from under the bed, and took a skull out of it. He stuffed the eye-sockets with silver paper and covered the teeth with it as well. He went out into the corridor, threw the scattered potatoes into the box. On top of them he put the skull, jaws open, and closed the lid.

He lay down—and read St John Chrysostome.

. . . .

Nadya was lying beside her husband, weeping.

I don't love him, I don't love him! Oh, how awful it is! When Philip went away I felt it bitterly, and yet things became easier, but now it's so dreary—I can't b-e-a-r it! Where is he, my dearest, my darling! What good is this flat to me, and this husband and all this money! I'm alone—and there's n-o-o Philip!

Her husband never said an unnecessary word. He worked in a secret establishment. As a locksmith, perhaps? The palms of his hands were covered with corns, like concrete, you couldn't pierce them with a needle.

Philikins, my dearest, do help me! Send me a post-card, I know you're not having an easy time either, perhaps you're dead already . . .

Her husband snored and stirred in his sleep. Nadya was

trying to control herself, her head was tossing on the pillow—but she could not bear it and began to sob.

"Nadya, what's the matter, darling, what's happened?"

Her husband's hand, like a flat-iron, travelled over her face.

"Nothing, Grisha, nothing, it just came over me. Go to sleep."

Grigori did not go to sleep.

What could be the matter? He wondered: had he offended her somehow? It didn't seem so. He'd come back from work late—the meeting had dragged on. It had been a very important one, and there was a terrible lot of work, he was tired. And his wife hadn't even smiled at him, although that didn't really matter. The children were quite all right. Hm. Had she fallen in love with someone? Or was she thinking of her first husband?

Grigori Brandov felt uncomfortable and vexed.

Of course, Petatorov had been a well-educated man, she'd had a more interesting life with him. Why did she marry me? I'm a simple man, but I look after my family, and it didn't even enter that mad philologist's head to do that.

The flat, my salary—they're no worse than that of any Academic, the kids are getting bigger—the eldest is his, that fool's . . . What more can she want? Well nothing, really . . . It's true, there's something of Petatorov about him. He came and asked me: why do we have such a ponderous name—Brandov?[1] I lost my temper, shouted at him . . .

[1] Brandov is a German name, with a Russian ending added (*Tr. note*).

But Nadya is weeping.

You've shut yourself up in a shell, she says, away from me. But how can I help it, if that's the sort of work I have? Yes, I work as an official applauder! Too bad if that sort of work is despised by some people! I feed my wife and children! And I love my work, yes I do! When, the day after an important meeting I read the words: (*applause*), (*loud applause*), (*prolonged applause*) printed in the paper in bold type—I'm happy! I too have contributed my little bit! My work is highly valued, which means, people need me! My salary goes up every year, the demand for our applauding toilers' hands is growing! As society progresses, we occupy more and more places in the hall—we know how to clap better than others. I'm already head of a clappers' brigade, soon I'll get promotion; in a year's time I'll graduate from the Higher Applause School, without interruption of normal work. Then all paths will be open, even . . . it's frightening to think . . .

Brandov was dropping off to sleep.
Nadya was weeping.

Petatorov cried out in his sleep, and the cat never left his side, keeping watch in the room, ready in case of danger to give warning: "Miaou!" Her eyes were as green as neon grapes in a shop window.

Sheptunov was reading St John Chrysostome.

Chapter 5

In the Zoo

Petatorov had lain low. He had not gone out for about two weeks, resting in hopeless sobriety. He lay on his bed, smoked—and meditated. The landlady grumbled about Phil's frivolous habits—instead of trying to find some money he was reading books! And he only ventured out to fetch firewood from the yard. Outside it was winter, with snow and blizzards, sometimes with slush. Hunched up, Philip sat in front of the stove and looked at the blue flame in its depths, at the hottest point. He helped the old woman make her soup, in exchange for which he got a meal. The three of them ate together: the landlady, Petatorov and the cat. When the meal was over Phil would move over to the stove, the cat would join him, and they would sit and chat for hours.

"Puss, do you love me?" Petatorov asked on one occasion.

The cat looked down modestly, her little pink nose blushed.

"A woman never answers: I don't love you," she whispered, "but I do like you very much. It's true that I also love Vaska the tom, he and I see a lot of each other. Alas! We can't live together—my landlady would never agree to having a tom here as well! I'm so unhappy, Phil!" The cat sobbed.

"Oh, don't cry, Puss," said Petatorov, touched. "The main thing is that you love each other!"

"Yes, of course, but I do so much want to have a family life!"

Petatorov went to his room, and lay down on the mattress.

Snow is lying outside . . . But I'm warm here. There's nothing I want now.

. . . And I understand: it can't be otherwise. It's difficult to endure all that, I wasn't able to. I became a person, and, it seems, must die. It's time! What difference does it make if I do it myself, or if others help me? Ah, Nadezhda! We could have been sitting in one cage, feasting our eyes on each other. Why did we run away in different directions? And now we are perishing . . .

Very well. Come what may—so be it.

. . . I'm simply afraid of dying slowly—too slowly. Who's afraid of the Last Judgment accompanied by the hallooing and whistling of archangels? God has decided that a quick death is easy, the trial started long ago, and the accused were born and live in the dock. As yet they are suffering under a delusion.

Rise up in revolt, Phil!

If I knew how to walk on my hands, everything would be different . . .

Perhaps I should go to Paris? . . .
—Ha! Ha! Ha!
Yes . . .

Petatorov was drinking tea—black and bitter. Life was becoming better, more cheerful.

Op-pa!
I'll go . . . and look for . . . work! . .
At the cemetery or the zoo—whichever's easier.

. . . .

On Monday Brandov arrived at work earlier than usual in order to catch the head of the Applause Section. Gena, the porter, pretending not to recognize Brandov, scrutinized his pass for a long time. Grigori was not indignant —that was the procedure, it was secret work. In the vast courtyard helicopter propellers were rotating noisily, people were bustling about, helping each other on with their parachute packs.

A commando of applauders was about to leave.

"Where are you flying to, Pasha?" Brandov shouted to a foreman he knew.

"To Saratov!"

"Happy clapping to you."

Brandov went down a long corridor and glanced into the rest room. The brigade on duty was playing dominoes. "Hallo, clappers!" Grigori shouted. "Hullo—hullo! What's new?" "Same as ever." "Well, thank goodness for that." Brandov loved being at work: people treated him with warmth and respect, behind his back they would say: "He's one of us, a real clapper!" Brandov gave a cursory glance at his beloved wall-newspaper *For All Out Clapping*, to which he contributed, and to which he sent in cartoons. For that issue too he had drawn a caricature of Pendyulin who, at a meeting, had missed the foreman's signal and had started to applaud later than was indicated in the scenario. Pendyulin was represented with huge ears and little tiny hands. The inscription under the drawing read: "You must clap with your hands, not with your ears."[1] Everyone had laughed, even Tumbov, the head of the department, had roared with laughter. On the walls hung diagrams and placards, aids to improve applauding skill: disembodied hands, clapping at a certain angle and at a certain force; incorrect, erroneous ways of clapping, crossed out with a red cross. Brandov read through the painfully familiar slogans: "He who does not clap, does not eat," "Clap quicker than anyone, better than anyone, more cheerfully than anyone."

Oh! They'd put up the results of the competitions . . . let's see, let's see . . ." First place, for the number of hours clapped: S. V. Sluchivshiysya's brigade, which has been given the challenge penant . . ." They've done better than us, the devils!

"But we're a magnificent lot!" thought Brandov with pride. "We spare neither hands nor health! And yet people have tried to slander us: you clapped and clapped, people said, and when the first bomb fell in '41 no one heard it! Slanderers! Had they counted the sleepless nights spent over *A Short Course in the Art of Applauding*?![2] But they pass us by, there's been no promotion for a long time . . . Pre-war clappers have got on in the world, become bosses, and we're just clappers, as we've always been. There's no justice, is there?"

[1] The Russian expression "to clap with your ears" means to listen to something without taking in what is being said (*Tr. note*).
[2] Allusion to *A Short History of the CPSU* (*Tr. note*).

Sima Minuetov, his assistant for spitting on the palms of the hands, came up to Brandov and whispered:

"Pendyulin's thesis 'On the Role of Applause Organizations during the Transitional Period' has been accepted! He's now got a Ph.D in Applause, and he's going off to teach at the University!"

"That's a blow," thought Brandov.

"And what's more," Minuetov went on, "the Bawlers have broken Petka Molierov's nose, they're bragging that they'll thrash us all!"

Brandov flushed crimson. What! They were insulting people from his brigade! They were causing them moral damage! And yet, ahead lay responsible work—several congresses, the elections. No team spirit whatsoever.

Thanks, Sima, let's go and have a word with them!"

The Public Criers' department was situated one floor lower. The Bawlers (as the clappers referred to the Public Criers), despised them and played dirty tricks on them as much as possible, probably because the Bawlers had been clappers once, and then had gone up in the world and now belonged to the "At the Workers' Request" department. They were better paid, and owing to the unhealthy conditions of production at work they received free milk. In spite of the fact that they were relatively few in number, they hectored the clappers, and sang a scurrilous song:

. . . .

. . . .

. . . .

. . . .

However the clappers did not leave this unanswered and would yell, as they walked past the hated department:

. . . .

. . . .

. . . .

. . . .

In the good old days the clappers and the public criers used to meet in the yard to sort out their quarrels—each side arms linked, with stakes and cobble stones. But the authorities had forbidden duels, even collective ones. Their animosity had gone underground.

"Actually, in what way is a public crier's work more estimable than ours?" Brandov said to himself. "I agree that they're on duty under the Praesidium table, I agree that they sit in the dust, until someone slips them a Resolution or a list of candidates, I agree they have to crawl to the door in a camouflage overall the colour of the platform, I agree they pelt along the corridor and into the hall. And from there they shout: I propose, I nominate . . .! They vote the same as we do, but have to shout at the end: Long live this, long live that! Glory to so and so! And they are the first to strike up the Party anthem, they've got a splendid choir, you can't deny them that. At amateur concerts they always sing better than anyone else."

Without knocking, Brandov opened the door of the enemy department and went in accompanied by Sima. The public criers were sleeping on tables and benches, while in the neighbouring room they were rehearsing "laughter in the hall".

The public criers' brigade leader rose to meet the two clappers.

"Now what's all this about, Comrade Marfov?" said Brandov. "There's so much work ahead, and you go and smash Molierov's nose?"

Ha-ha-ha-ha-ha-ha-ha! could be heard through the wall.

"I personally have not smashed any nose, and this is the first time I've heard Molierov's nose mentioned," replied Marfov with dignity, in his beautiful sonorous voice.

"Molierov reported to me that one of your . . ."

"Drochetov!" prompted Minuetov.

". . . exactly, Drochetov broke his nose yesterday in the lavatory."

Oh! Oh! Hee-hee-hee-hee-hee-hee, ho ho ho ho ho ho, oh, haa-ha-ha!

"I'll look into it," said the hostile brigade leader with feigned concern. "If it is so, I shall punish the guilty person."

"I would ask you to warn all your men . . . that they should stop squaring personal accounts! There's a Congress coming on!"

Ha ha, hee hee! ha! ha! ha! haha, ah, hee, hee, hoho hohoho, ha!

"Vanya, stop a minute, our friends are here!"

Marfov knocked on the wall. The laughter ended abruptly. "My dear Grigori Brandov, you certainly needn't worry! I'll order Drochetov to issue the victim with three roubles for medical care," and he smiled venomously.

Brandov flushed.

"We don't need tips! Good-bye."

The clappers left, banging the door loudly.

"Sima," said the brigade leader. "Nip up to the office and take down the wall newspaper; we'll issue a new one today with congratulations to Pendyulin. Good lad! He's got a doctorate already!"

A minute later Brandov went into Tumbov's office. The latter clapped in sign of welcome, and then became totally absorbed in the sheet of paper which Brandov held out to him.

"Memorandum. The organization of our work has not

been sufficiently thought out. In response to the leadership's appeals, I have joined in the fight to economise state funds. In order to improve our work I propose the following: to use apes as applauders, but *especially*—for exclamations of approval. It is all the more important to train replacements for the old personnel, at the time when the question of new personnel is coming up again and again. I am convinced that the apes will carry out with credit the work entrusted to them. The training and purchase of a fresh batch of apes will soon pay for itself, thanks to the reduction in the staff of clappers. I append an estimate."

The scheme interested the boss, and he approved it.

"Put it into effect!" he said, as a parting shot.

Brandov was appointed head of an experimental group and issued with documents entitling him to work with apes.

"Nadya," said Brandov, on his return from work one day, 'Wouldn't you like to go to the Zoo tomorrow? It's ages since you and I went anywhere!"—the brigade leader smiled, squeezing Nadya in a steel embrace.

Nadya felt a lump in her throat. Her husband was inviting her to go somewhere! It was the second time in the three years they had been together. A long time ago, when they had first met, Grigori had invited her to a ceremonial evening dedicated to the memory of someone or other. Nadya had gone to it joyfully, thinking it was going to be good entertainment, but afterwards had cursed herself for going. For three hours someone on the platform had read out old newspaper cuttings, and to relieve the monotony a couple of fellows had appeared on the stage, had wheezed something on a minute accordion, and sung humorous songs about scrap metal; Nadya had felt tired, but Grigori had clapped deafeningly and had enjoyed himself. And now suddenly—he was proposing the zoo . . .

"I'll go!" she said, and smiled.

"Tomorrow at 12.00," said the brigade leader.

. . . .

Petatorov arrived at Presnya at about noon. Now, if he could only get fixed up here as a watchman or a keeper—how peaceful that would be! Apparently there still existed in the world wild animals which did not indulge in politics. *They* had not poked their ubiquitous fingers in here yet.

"I'm going to the personnel office," said Petatorov to the woman selling tickets. She forced open her eyelids with difficulty and glanced at the big clock by the Underground. As soon as she closed her eyes again, Petatorov darted over the fence. It was warmer today, the mud squelched under his feet. A grey day. Ducks were quacking, mist was rising over the unfrozen part of the pond, birds were twittering behind the wire-netting. How calm it was here. He sat down on a bench and took out his flask. He had a drink and a smoke.

If only he could hide here for ever, so that no one knew and no one saw him. Abdicate from all his past and present. Quietly and inconspicuously guard the tigers. In the evenings he would read Ovid and be carried away to an ancient and sunny land; he would wander through the crowd of Athenians and Romans and drink wine. And then be banished, and pine away on the seashore: not like nowadays, but sublimely, and in hexametres. Undoubtedly a beautiful girl would appear too, and he would love her, and catch fish for her in the clear water.

"Ah!" said Petatorov, and walked on. Ahead of him a pony was trotting in a circle. Philip quickened his step, the pony stopped—they were feeding it.

The pony did not look at anyone—they were always the same, there was no one to look at.

"It's been trotting like that for more than twenty-six years," said the woman-keeper. "Go on, eat it up, you good for nothing!"

The pony munched half-heartedly and did not finish its bread. They put a sullen, pimply boy in the little carriage, and the pony trotted off again, grey and calm.

Petatorov, who was walking across clay, slipped; he was going to the apes. The monkey-house was situated opposite the antelope house, on the other side of a pool.

A pungent smell of wool and warmth crept up Philip's nose, while the loud howl of the monkey choir greeted him. Behind the bars languished unrecognized champions of gymnastics, jumping about.

"Va-vo-va-kuaaaoo!!"

"Good morning, my dears!" thought Petatorov. In the corner cage sat his old friend Manon. She was picking over bits of food in a melancholy way—white bread, segments of apples, boiled eggs—and listlessly dropping them.

"Manon!" called an attendant. The monkey looked at him and rushed to the top of the cage, revealing her blood-red horny hind-quarters.

"The public is rather second-rate," thought Philip. "Look at that woman over there, with her puffy face, a moron."

"I'll show you! I'll show you!" the woman was saying in a whisper, wagging her finger at Manon. "I'll show you!"

A man in a good coat and with well-pressed trousers stopped beside Philip.

"Those wouldn't do," he muttered. "They're too small, it would be too obvious . . . But they don't shout badly, you can hear a ring of triumph. No, no, we must have chimpanzees, or ourang-outangs—bigger ones, it'll be easier to make them up . . ."

Petatorov listened, astonished.

"But their arses, their arses are good! If one were to clap on them! One monkey could do the work of five . . ." The man began slapping his buttocks. "Splendid!"

Scared country cousins were resting beside the cages, after the grandiose sights of the capital. The monkeys looked familiar to them, like drunks outside a beer hall in Penza.

"Lying down, are you?" they were saying to a macaco. "Well, you lie there, then, hee-hee! They give you food and drink—what more d'you want, ha ha."

"A lot of work will have to be put into them," the well-dressed visitor was saying to himself. "They're not well-grounded in ideology. We'll manage it, we'll give them ideological education, we've managed harder cases than that. Ah, what splendid arses! Pity it's unethical— just imagine, if a delegate suddenly started jumping up and slapping his arse. What would our dear foreign guests think! It's impossible. I'll recruit some chimpanzees and ourang-outangs, I'll put them in little suits— Pavlov's Reflexes—I'll go and get some advice—we'll work it all out, and full steam ahead in the name of the radiant future. You'll be promoted to senior clapper, Brandov! You're a good fellow, you are!"

Petatorov went away from the monkeys and saw: BEASTS OF PREY.

Ah, just what I need.

The beasts of prey were lying down, only the hyena was running around the cage.

The hyena was incensed by the injustice of it all. Fancy sitting here in prison, without trial or investigation, while others were free, going about their business.

And suddenly the puma gave a terrifying yowl, and her visceral howl was answered by the lion.

Silence. Urine murmured in the trough beside the cages, like a brook in springtime.

Beeside the bro-o-ok a youth-ful drea-mer
Was plucking flow-ers to make a wre-ath . . .
oh, what a thing to remember.

At the end of the building a keeper was sitting dozing over his newspaper.

"Puss, puss!" said Petatorov to the ocelot, a beautiful wild cat. The ocelot climbed on to a dry tree stump in the cage and rubbed its little nose against a branch.

"Not very talkative!" thought the professor and called again: "Puss, puss!"

"You're teasing it—don't," said the keeper.

"But I just wanted to talk to it a bit."

The keeper yawned.

"That's how you all start, and then you go and play some trick or other."

"I shan't do anything," said Petatorov.

"I know you! You'll go and do something, and it's me who'll have to answer for it."

"I swear I won't do anything," Petatorov assured him.

"I bet! About ten years ago someone just like you used to come here, and studied and examined . . . and then . . . You haven't anything to drink with you, have you?"

Petatorov took out his flask and gave it to the keeper. The old man took a gulp, spat, and amicably invited Philip to sit beside him on the bench.

The legend of the black panther

Ten years ago we had a black panther living in this cage here, together with a serval; we all called the panther Shura. Beautiful she was—with black fur, her whole pelt shone; well, all black panthers are like that, but she had a distinctive white stripe round her neck, like the imprint of a noose. She was gentle, but one day, when a small plank had rotted away in the partition, the serval—the mate of the female we have now—stuck its paw through into the panther's cage. And she bit off its paw and ate it. The serval was ill for a long time and then died of blood poisoning. Look how restless its mate is! Yes . . . The panther, apparently, was only pretending to be gentle. At that time I blamed her, but there was nothing you could do about it. The panther just lay there for days on end—oh! and how black she was! If you went up to her, she'd turn her face round, but you couldn't make out her eyes—the whole of her shone so. She'd turn away just as if you weren't there. But she realized the situation she was in. For example, if the cage had to be washed—you'd open the door into the neighbouring cage, which was empty, and she'd move into it of her own accord, you only had to say: "Shura!"

She didn't have much of an appetite, no, I can't say she
had. If you threw her half a leg, she wouldn't budge,
but at night you'd hear: crunch, crunch. So she must
have been eating. In the daytime she used to lie with her
back to all the visitors and occasionally she'd give a
sigh. If you called to her: "Shura!"—she'd thump the
ground with her tail, once, and that's all—as if to say,
what d'you want? And it was then that a fellow took
to visiting us, about fifty years old he was. He used to
come and look at my wild beasties. As soon as he saw
the panther, he took to her, he used to sit on the barrier
for about four hours at a stretch and never move. And
what d'you think—she began to notice him. They'd sit
and look at each other, as if they'd fallen in love. One
day I went up to him and asked him: "Who are you?"
And he said: "I'm a scientist, an ornithologist," and
shoved some paper or other under my nose. "Very well,"
I said, "look at her, study her, only you just be careful
with the panther: she's quiet, but she's fierce. You
probably realize all this better than we do, you know
this beast's habits." I felt happier in my mind, and they
spent half the winter sitting there like that: the panther
gazed at him through the bars of her cage, while he sat
outside on the barrier, saying something or other to her.
Once I heard him whispering: "You're a free bird . . . not
a bird of prey, no, a bird of the air! Don't grieve. Life's
like that: a cub grows up—and in he goes—into a cage!"
The panther listened attentively, and it was almost as if
her face became kinder; she lay there, not taking her
eyes off the ornithologist. They used to have long talks
sometimes, and the panther seemed to argue: she would
growl something or other. The ornithologist was called
Yashka. I got used to him, he helped me clean the cage,
carry round the fodder. And we made soup of the tigers'
meat, not of their own meat, of course, but if you take
a kilo from their day's ration of 100 kilos—it isn't

noticed. We'd sit and eat, Yashka wasn't talkative, he would only talk to Shura. That winter, not many visitors came here, he and I would sit here and had the wild beasts to ourselves. I used to rely on him, I thought love of science made for carefulness. And I allowed myself to sleep peacefully. One night I went to sleep, although that's contrary to regulations. When I woke up in the morning to hand over to the next man on duty—no Yashka, I looked here, there, had he gone home, or what? I went up to Shura—and there was the ornithologist in her cage! I started trembling—that's the end of Yashka, I thought! He was sitting in the cage, stroking her face, while Shura was purring and fawning on him. "Come out, Yashka," says I, "while you're still in one piece!" "I don't want to," he replied. I opened the passage into the neighbouring cage, so as to drive the panther in there—she didn't go! I tried to push her with a hook—she grasped the iron with her teeth, pulled it out of my hands! And how she snarled! Such a snarl I had never heard from a captive beast in all my life! "Yashka," I screamed, "don't be a fool! Come out! If you don't, I'll call the fire brigade, they'll take you out by force; there'll be one hell of a row!" But there was Shura, standing at the bars and snarling at me with a terrible growl. "Don't take it to heart, Vanya," says the ornithologist. "I've made a great discovery of world-wide importance: your Shura isn't a panther at all, she's a bird! A new species, not discovered until now." I listened to him for a bit, and then called in the fire-brigade. The chaps came and started driving Shura away with boathooks—the ornithologist wouldn't let them, threw himself at the iron hooks. We played the hose pipes on them, they both went together under the jet. And the wild beasts didn't half kick up a din— they roared and raved! "Well, then, to hell with them!" said the firemen, "when the Director comes he'll deal with it." In the morning Mikhailych rushed in, quite pale, ticked me off—and went to Shura. She was lying down, Shura was; and the ornithologist in floods of tears was sitting in front of her, stroking her face. "Oh, my little bird, the like of which has never been seen, my joy, when we get out of here—we'll fly off to distant lands . . ." The Director tried this and that with the ornithologist—Yashka wouldn't come out. "I've found my happiness," says he, "and my vocation, this," says he, "is my place in life." They decided to shoot the panther. A famous marksman came with a sniper's rifle, and took up his position, but it was hardly a difficult shot—the cage wasn't more than five metres long. At that Yashka takes out a little knife and says quietly: "if you," says he, "perpetrate such a crime, I shall immediately plunge this knife into my heart." Again things didn't work out, and we were afraid to stop giving meat to Shura, in case she got hungry and munched up the ornithologist. We worried for about five days, and then we had an idea: we put poison in her ration. She died. Yashka wept and wept! The firemen got into the cage, and we pulled at him, but he caught hold of Shura's paws and we couldn't tear him away, try as we might. So we pulled him out with the carcass. They had to saw off the panther's paws—after all, you couldn't break his arms. The animals went mad, the puma was hoarse, its eyes flashed—that's all. Mm, yes . . . They put Yashka in a car. He never let go of the paws, stroked his face with them and cried. They took him away to the proper place. Yes . . . You see, we get all sorts here, don't be cross that I shouted at you."

They had another sip each. Petatorov quickly left. He was distressed and suddenly felt uncertain whether they would let him out. The high fence of the zoo was visible from wherever one was, and Philip had the impression of being in a huge open-air cage.

Must escape from here. Ah, you geese and swans! Swimming about, are you? Swans, they've fattened you up. You haven't got a neck—it's a leg in a downy stocking. And you must have forgotten your swan song. You eat-rest-eat. And you don't need wide open spaces any more. You eat white bread, you're a bit too heavy to fly. You splash about and dive, well-fed and snow-white. Swan songs would be simply out of place, they would be taken for bad manners, for a *defamatory* song. Very well, one needn't take any notice of sauce spilled on a tablecloth.

Petatorov looked sideways—a swan was gliding along the bank—and caught sight of a woman. She was standing about twenty paces away, leaning on the cold iron railing. Phil saw a half-forgotten black coat and black boots.

I must . . . can that really be Nadya? No . . . she didn't have a scarf like that . . . must go away without being noticed. Stealthily.

Without realizing it, Petatorov edged towards the woman.

If she doesn't turn round . . . no . . . it's not Nadya . . . quiet, Phil. Don't let your shoes squelch, Professor.

. . . .

Verily it passes all understanding how it comes about that God's enemies and offenders enjoy sunshine and rain, and all the other blessings of God. The men enjoying all this are those who after spiritual meat, after such great blessings, after listening to innumerable exhortations, surpass the beasts by their cruelty, rise up against each other and defile their tongue by slandering their neighbour. And so, thinking on this, let us cast the poison out of our hearts, let us destroy enmity, let us extol. . .

Sheptunov laid aside St John Chrysostome and stood at the door. A familiar lisping could be heard in the corridor. The cardboard of the box was rustling.

"Not zo lout, he might hear!"

"Senya, vat a big vun! Must be a cabbage!"

"Let's have a look."

"Philip!"

Petatorov turned his head.

Two eyes and a mouth flashed.

Aaaaaa!—howled the old woman and dropped the skull.

"Ah!" Petatorov covered his face with his hands.

"It's you, Philipkin!"

A company of Red Army soldiers swept through the corridor.

Sheptunov scratched himself with a sense of satisfaction and lay down again.

"Nadezhda!"

Petatorov was trembling. He looked at the woman's face, at the shiny fur coat—and trembled.

Nadya took a step forward—her eyes were quite close. Oh, Lord.

"Philipkin!" said Nadya. "Have we really met?!"

"Yes," said Petatorov. "We have."

"Why did we part, Philip?"

"I don't know."

"Say something, Philip!"

"Yes. I must say something."

"Oh, these years! I'm dying without you, Philip! I don't love my husband, or my children, because you're not with me! I looked for you, and I couldn't find you!"

"Even the police can't," muttered Petatorov.

"You've made an empty husk of me, Philipkin! I was living, then *you came*, and then went away, and now I can't go on as I used to."

"Nadyenka! Let's go away from here, shall we?"

They made their way slowly to the exit, and then tramped along the slushy street, feeling frozen. They came across a flower shop and warmed themselves, surrounded by cacti and orchids.

"And now, Philipkin, nothing can be changed. Take me with you, we'll be together. I'll give up everything, ah, everything! What I'll give up is *nothing*, you need me, do you think I don't see it? Without me, you'll perish."

"Yes. Only you alone show any affection for me. Whatever rough millstones turn inside me and grind me, now you have touched them and stopped them with one little finger. Too late! . . . I am nobody now, Nadyenka. I don't work, I've nowhere to live, nothing to eat."

"I know. And all the same—apart we'll both die. But together—you madman!—we'll survive, in spite of everything, in spite of these people, in spite of all! Ah, Phil, do agree, do agree! What will our death prove, and to whom?"

"Comrades, this is not the place to clarify your personal relations," said the shop girl.

And once more they walked through the slushy snow and sat in a café: and talked and talked.

"Nadyenka, you want to be the straw for me to clutch at! At this moment I'm happy, you can't imagine my happiness! *Petatorov* is needed! That's so preposterous, that I'm happy. But I have only one destiny . . ."

"No!" cried Nadya, so loudly that even the waiters turned round. "Our destiny is to survive and conquer! Believe me, Philipkin! I'll be with you, we'll endure everything, can this nightmare really last for centuries, no, no, people will understand, you're not alone! *You're not alone*! Call out and people will come, rise up in revolt!"

"Rise in revolt?!" said Petatorov tensely. "And then—what? They'd crush us, and if we were to do the crushing—then what? I've become crafty."

"We have a son, growing up . . ." said Nadya.

Petatorov felt embarrassed.

"Well, and how is . . . he?"

"Just like you. Always reading books, doesn't say much. Sometimes, when he's not expecting it, I look at him and say: Andrey!—he gives a start: Yes, Mummy? —I told him about you—everything. He made a face and said: a decadent!"

Petatorov felt bitterly offended.

"Yes, yes, Nadyenka, I . . ."

'Philipkins, ah Philip!"

". . . have sunk very low, Nadezhda."

"Forgive me, darling, let's go home quickly, Philipkin!"

Damp snow clung to their faces and weighed down their eyelashes, they hid in a doorway, and Philip sensed her lips, ran his fingers through her hair, and his lips wandered over her face—a wayfarer, dying in the desert from thirst and uncanny cold in the marrow of his bones.

"Nadezhda, do you hear—the drums are beating . . . no, it's the bells, we're parting. Nadya, *now*, *this minute* we are parting, I must be taken away, it's no good joining me, Nadyenka! I was sitting on a beach and took handfuls of sand—it flowed through my fingers and disappeared. I'm ill, Nadya, forgive me!"

"Philip, we'll collect your son and go away! We're paupers, but is that so terrible?"

Petatorov was seeing Nadya home, they kissed in a gateway, he was dumbfounded: a vagabond who, beneath a heap of dirty rags, had glimpsed tender, loving lips. Caressing fingers stroked his chapped face, with his lips he pressed her palms, he rocked like a boat, he saw love—and did not notice that the sun was setting. Fingers sped over lips, went up over cheeks, and forded eyes. His eyelashes plied up and down like the oars of galley slaves. They were rowing out of the storm, but a wave overtook them and overwhelmed them—Nadya felt Petatorov was weeping. And she was horrified: was he, Philip, really weeping?!

"Phil, what's the matter?"

"Goodbye, Nadya, I'm not what you need, I myself am drowning! Good-bye! Look after . . . our little boy, won't you?"

"I will, I will . . . yes, yes . . ."

"Nadyenka? D'you hear, Nadyenka—they're ringing the bells . . . We're parting, I know. But who has devised it all, Nadyezhda, who?! I've collapsed, I'm a fragment off a temple, don't kiss it, aah! What's the point of flogging a sphinx with a lash, what's the point, Nadezhda! He'll raise his dead head—and let it fall on his paws! Nadyenka!"

The professor lost all sense of reality and was kissing Nadya's weeping eyes—she pressed herself to him, he carried her up the steps of a staircase—where to?! His hand did not feel the cold in the warm bends behind her knees—he ran past houses and gateways.

Snow, driving snow, carrying all before it, and Philip running with Nadya in his arms, the blizzard is whirling, and her face is close to him. Nadya is asleep, she does not remember the path of their flight, flies as if on wings —flies in Petatorov's arms, and the snow clings and covers Nadya's face, and it does not melt any more!

"Nadezhda! Nadya-aaa!"

"What, dearest?" Nadezhda stirred, and two arms— vine tendrils—twined round his cold neck, and Petatorov sensed their warmth.

"Are you tired, dearest? Put me down . . ."

They were running, the blizzard was overtaking him, and the snowstorm whirled around them, snakes of snow clutched at their feet, the blizzard whistled and rustled.— Hey, Nadya! What is the matter with you? Brandov is waiting for you, your lawful . . . aaaa . . .

Nadya fell into a snowdrift, they laughed, and Peta- torov heard with amazement his own happy laugh— sadly barking, and Nadya laughed, like a bell weeping as it tinkled in the midst of a snowy field. She clung to Petatorov's shoulder for support as she emptied the snow from her boot, while he looked at the familiar little bump by her thumb—the snowstorm was blowing in gusts of powder, and twined itself round steps, and piled up sorrow in drifts along the streets, and sorrow shrouded windows, and lamps, and eyes, the blizzard smothered happiness with snow, and blinded Philip Petatorov.

Now he was walking mechanically, and there was nothing he needed, except to fall asleep on dry, warm bedding. Philip had become wooden, and Nadezhda was frightened—like an insane Magdalene, she was kissing a wooden Christ, taken off a cross in a church.

"No-no, no-no," she was saying, standing there in an attitude of utter despair. "Philip! This isn't you! Come to life, my beloved!"

The professor stood there, a curtain of needle-shaped icicles hung between them, his face was fading out, while Nadezhda disappeared in the raging storm.

Then Petatorov spread out his arms, and a white cross swayed in the blizzard.

Is the cup full? But they will not fail to offer it to me. I'm alone in the whole world, they will not make a mistake. It is *my* destiny to drink of it . . . How did you do it, Socrates? At least you were warm, in sunny Greece . . .

Petatorov fell, cross-shaped, on the snow, a little cloud of cold down rose and covered him.

". . . iiiliii! . . . iiilii!"—someone shouted from the other end of the world, while snowy hands dragged him down into an icy pit—to bury him, freeze him!

"Here comes drunken death," thought the professor. "Rise up against it, Phil."

"Whaaaat for . . ." sang the blizzard. "You're a-a-a-l-l riiight . . ."

"The cat will die of hunger without me," objected

Petatorov, and he stirred; a layer of snow fell off his back.

"The cat will die," he murmured and got up, sliding his hands along the lamp-post. "She's got no other home, the cat . . ."

From lamp-post—to lamp-post, from house—to house, Petatorov wandered off to Sokolniki.

Chapter 6

Nativity

Petatorov slept through more than twenty-four hours without any disturbing dreams. His brain was resting, hiding away his sorrows in the depths of his soul, his wounds were healing, leaving scars behind them, like a crust of ice formed overnight in water-filled hoofmarks of cattle.

The cat was miaouing; she had seized the collar of his coat in her little teeth, and pulled it off Petatorov's head. Philip sneezed, rubbed his face and said:

"Stop it! Let me sleep, can't you?"

"How much longer will you sleep?" asked the cat, indignantly.

Petatorov was waking up. And he had a feeling of extraordinary happiness and peace. He had not yet opened his eyes, joy seethed in and around him—after his long, salutary rest. He stretched out his hand to find a cigarette, and the cat grasped it in her paws, rubbed her nose against it and purred.

"Puss!" said Petatorov, feeling even happier; a Japanese picture—serene and beautiful—flowered in his mind. He opened his eyes: a wisp of cigarette smoke was hanging in the air, as over the volcano Fuji Yama.

"If only this happiness doesn't get spoiled—if I live carefully, don't trample on this little shoot, give it time to become stronger, and then we'll grow together, I'll pro . . ."

"Phil! When will you give me the rent?" asked the landlady through the door.

"Soon!"

". . . tect it! Lord, I'm happy just at this very moment, like this. If only I don't upset this happiness, don't destroy it. I'll sleep a lot, read a lot, if only I could gradually be reborn, get back energy and strength, I'd take Nadya and Andrey, we'd manage it somehow. But we mustn't sink into the mire, we mustn't succumb to love of comfort. I am the Honoured[1] Pauper of the Republic. 'We are gradually advancing . . .' But we're gradually getting besmirched, my dear Diogenes. People shout, looking into the darkness before them: Jacob is struggling with the angel. Are you sure it is Jacob? 'Jacob's getting the upper hand!'—The audience's attention has been distracted, and the crooks have it all their own way. Fish die in a poisoned stream—everyone weeps and struggles. People are trampled on—and the others are delighted, and scream: serve him right! You can't do that, my friends. What's the point in discussing the naturalness of the historical process? Or is your pain unnatural?!"

[1] "Honoured" is the title given in the USSR to workers who have gained the State's approval, e.g. "Honoured artist" (*Tr. note*).

That's where electrification has got us—pine-trees and bears all around . . .[1]

Petatorov was tired. The vision of Fuji Yama and the wise grey-haired Japanese waterfall had disappeared. Philip jumped up and limbered up a bit. The remnants of his muscles worked, throwing his body around the room.

"Good!" said Petatorov, tired by these physical exertions. He made himself some tea, and ate a few rusks which he dipped in it.

The empty feeling in the pit of my stomach seems to have gone. Out, must go out—find some work, collect Nadya. I've never had any energy—or determination to have any, for that matter. I have a desire for happiness—desire not to be a slave and not to be lonely . . . That— I have. Must find some work, where it's least trouble, at the cemetery, say. It's unlikely that Nadyenka would agree to live here, I don't want to myself, we'll have a light, clean room.

The landlady had gone out. Petatorov quickly ate a piece of boiled salt cod.

It's cold today. December, and there's a frost, and it's my birthday, and I've nothing to drink . . .

Philip went out, he was hurrying, while the frost, like

---

[1] An allusion to Lenin's famous slogan equating Communism to Soviet power plus electrification (*Tr. note*).

an accountant, was telling off his bones one by one. Steam poured from the doors of the Underground, red-cheeked girls and youths were rushing about with skis—they were out for a run, to have a rest, then at night in bed they would frolic and cuddle and purr together. At night we purr, in the daytime—we sing praises.

He made his way through little streets along which he had walked thousands of times; from afar he caught sight of a small church. The churchyard stretched out along the railway line; most likely as a mockery to its inhabitants. The station was teeming with luggage and Christmas trees.

Untrodden snow lay around the fence. Petatorov passed through the gates and, calm now, walked along the path, surrounded by crosses and tombstones. He knew many of the people who worked in the cemetery, they were friendly with him; as a matter of fact, it was impossible to quarrel and lose one's temper there: it was too quiet, too close to that sleepy man who comes the morning after a fancy-dress ball and clears up the broken china, sweeps away the gay little ribbons of paper streamers and the cigarette ends and mends the broken bits of parquet.

Snow lay on the trees, on the crosses, and in the crevices of the inscriptions. A black slab, upright over a grave, a broody angel sitting on top of it.

"He's cold," thought Petatorov. "Papusin, P. C. What a rare name."

He walked on and saw unpretentious little graves with hasty, unsure hand-written inscriptions, like graffiti on the wall of a school lavatory. "Oh Lord! Accept his mortal remains and give him peace." What does the Lord want his mortal remains for? It's illiterate. Oh, this one's better—"accept his soul". Here's another quite unobtrusive grave. Petatorov broke off a small branch and pushed the snow from the stone. "Libertova, E. F. Died tragically in the year . . ." A layer of granite had been chipped off, and Petatorov could not discover when exactly E. F. Libertova had died tragically. Probably her relatives had all died, no one was looking after the grave. It didn't matter to her.

Alongside Libertova was a strange burial vault—a little house with windows, which might have come from the playground of a kindergarten; outside it was carefully covered with wire-netting. Petatorov glanced inside: a little bench, a tiled floor, as in a bathroom, but instead of a bath there was, for some reason, a cross.

It would be nice to live here, if only one put in a stove, it's peaceful here. It wouldn't be bad to lie here, either. I'd be quite willing to lie here, there's no draught or snow.

He walked along the path, there were a great many graves: crosses, little mounds, gravestones covered with snow, fenced and unfenced, protected on all sides and above by railings—huge squirrel cages.

So many surnames, Christian names and patronymics. And all dead, all fated to end in the frosty ground. Why then do we bustle about on the surface? Ah, we protest, we're afraid, we intend to live . . .

"What's your name?" someone asked behind him.

Petatorov gave a start, and turned round. An old man, thick-set, in a short, shabby sheepskin coat; with the wadding coming out of his cap; a beard; twinkling brigand's eyes looking out from underneath bushy eyebrows. No gloves, a book under his arm.

"Why d'you want to know?"

"You can go up to anyone here and read who he was and when he lived. But you have to be asked, it's not written on your face."

"Philip Arkadyevich."

"I shall just call you Philip. You're young enough to be my son. Come along."

They went down the slope and reached the southern fence, beyond which began the municipal rubbish dump.

"There," said the old man, pointing to an obelisk built of marble blocks; a white oval portrait of a young man with a little beard was half erased. Where the blocks joined, the paint had peeled off, and the calm handsome face was now looking out from behind bars.

"Death has discovered the mystery of life, although, perhaps, by accident: his parents had enough money to hire a painter. But now read this, I've been turning things over in my mind a lot today."

Petatorov took the paper.

From their very birth on, people are imprisoned in frames. The child's bed (a cradle)—is a frame, which foreshadows their fate for them. They live within the frame of the house, the school, the family, the frame accompanies them everywhere. If they create something, then it is within the frame of generally accepted intentions, otherwise they will not be understood and they won't be given money. They grow old and die within a frame—they are put in a coffin and their life ends with a black framed announcement in the papers. There are people free of this frame—gypsies and those living in the mountains.

"And then we approach God, for He is infinite; feel Him, Philip. You are helpless because people take vengeance on you when they hear your words. God is even more helpless. He appeals to you, but you are deaf. Have you ever been happy, if only once?"

"I have, yes," said Petatorov, in a low voice. "I woke up—ages ago, in spring, day was breaking—and I saw beside me the face of the woman I loved."

"If only you could have turned your whole life into a morning like that, but you knew that that was impossible —and the thought poisoned you! Truth is happiness, happiness is love, so choose the most durable of all loves —love of God. However, God is an imprecise word for specifying the Self . . . Love will take up its abode in you and—will live in you."

"I can't believe even in God. I did try, old man, but nothing came of it . . ."

"You have not meditated enough. You wanted to find some kind of brother or friend, to find a strong and independent being, to whom you could say: Lord, it is You! He does not exist, Philip, learn to love nothingness! You wanted a correlation between yourself and the abyss,[1] you wanted to find in it a loving You. And you lost your way! Because you imagined that you were outside the abyss, that it stood before you—you are in it, Philip! Love it—it is all around, it alone is immutable, it has accepted you and does not disdain you; this is God."

"Why then did the abyss secrete man?"

"It also disgorged both the sea, and the stars just as it did the cells of your body, it secreted everything— therefore, it secreted *Nothingness*. Everything remained in it . . ."

"And what about the spirit, which torments us?"

"Are you certain that a stone, a tree, the sun are not tormented or are less tormented than you are? You are mistaken, Philip. Have you ever looked at the starry sky? Remember how awestruck you were, and how then peace

[1] "The void" would be a better translation of the original Russian word "bezdna"; but the accepted term in Cabbalistic theosophy is "the abyss".

filled you and lulled you, you felt the caress of the abyss and it was calling you and demanded only one thing: that you should recognize it!"

"Old man, you don't know the answer or else you are keeping something back . . ."

"Learn to love the abyss, Philip. It is as trusting as a child, you have betrayed it dozens of times, and yet all the same—you will come to it, and it will not reproach you for your long flight from it, it will receive Philip— as it will accept us all, it will listen with joy to a declaration of love. For you have belonged to it for a very long time, since long before your forefathers were born. You say that you are unhappy? Learn to love the abyss! Go, now!"

Philip was prey to an uneasy feeling as he slowly picked his way between the graves to the church. He went up to the side door and opened it, went down the narrow staircase into a small oblong room. An electric bulb cast a dim light; the sexton, wrapped in rags, was snoring on a bunk.

"Gryzha!" said Petatorov, and the shadow of a smile flitted across his face.

"Eh?" said the sexton in his sleep.

"Look out! They're building a crematorium!"

"You haven't got the right to!!"

Gryzha leapt up—he was shaggy, with his face oozing down towards his nose, which hung like a huge drop of red wine.

"Ah, Phil! . . . Hello, my dear fellow. All we have for company here is stones and creaking bones, hee-hee! Where've you blown in from?" They sat down to table with a child's coffin for a bench. Pickled cucumbers, potatoes, fresh bread and vodka—on seeing such abundance, Petatorov laughed. They had a drink, and a feeling of warmth stole through Philip's thin body.

"You haven't been here for a long time, Phil," said the sexton.

"I was busy. Gryzha, you wouldn't have some sort of little job going here, would you?"

"Not at the moment. Come again in spring, then there will be—we'll have to clear the rubbish off the plots, you can help us. It's winter, not everyone can scrape up enough cash to be buried in December. They aren't bringing many here."

"Pity," said Petatorov.

"Doesn't matter. No money, I dare say? Here's a rouble. Or, I know what, Phil," the sexton pointed to a skull, white with age, lying on the floor by a pile of spades. "We were digging the day before yesterday and found it. You could flog this Yorrick, couldn't you? You'd get about fifteen roubles, probably."

They drank in silence. It was warm in the sexton's room.

"And where are your mates?"

"Our Party Organizer's ill, they've gone to visit him in hospital. The others are in the club, playing in the orchestra."

"Gryzha, have you ever noticed an old man with a beard?"

"Whereabouts is the grave?"

"He's alive, he was talking to me today on the third plot."

"I don't remember . . . ah, yes, yes, with little plaits?[1] I've met him. He goes on about the abyss and showers abuse on the gravediggers. He's got a son buried here, a Colonel Kretov. Yes, I've seen him. He stops by the

---

[1] ". . . with little plaits". This possibly suggests a priest; Orthodox priests have long hair, which they sometimes wear plaited, especially at home. However, since the old man's ideas all derive from Jewish mysticism, it is more likely that the author means the ringlets (which are not plaited) of the Hesidim, and did not wish to make the allusion too obvious (*Tr. note*).

obelisk and hisses at it: 'You've shot your way out, you lousy scoundrel! You thought you'd have them all where you wanted them but there wasn't room to manœuvre—it's cramped, the abyss! Anyway, you're dead now, had your chips. And you, grave diggers,' he says, 'you clothe corpses in wood and stone, you've set up a whole studio, you parasites, to screen the abyss from people's eyes!' I laugh and say: 'You'd do better to help us dig, father, instead of stamping about here. I'll give you a drink.' He starts shouting and screaming and kicking up a shindy; 'give me a spade, you scoundrel,' he says and—into a grave he jumps. He has a drink and a bite—and then he preaches about the abyss again until he falls asleep . . . Well now, you come in the spring, Phil, and I'll fix you up. Or, what about this: in the undertakers' department there are foreign language and needlework groups being organized, isn't that your line?"

"Why foreign languages?"

"The bosses know best."

"I don't want to teach."

"Perhaps you'd like to have a nap, Phil?"

"I'd better be on my way."

"Drop in in the spring, it's nice here: the birds sing, the sun shines . . ."

Gryzha lay down on the bunk and wrapped himself up in his rags.

Petatorov went away and disappeared into the city. He pondered on the old man and the abyss and could not reconcile himself to his uselessness in this world. He wandered about the cold streets, and spent nights in the upper stories of huge new buildings; he would wrap himself up in his coat and lie there, snuggled up to the warm side of a radiator. If he failed to fall asleep, he would amble over to the railway station; it was not so lonely there. He would chat with old men who had come to the city for their son's wedding, or to present a petition to the Supreme Soviet. They would air their grievances to him, complain, expect advice on how to ask for something so as to get some sort of result. Petatorov would sympathize, he would begin to feel better as if he were no longer alone, and yet he was quite unable to find a positive aim, for the sake of which he could try to *start living*. He thought of Nadya, Andrey—and could not find in himself the strength to hope; grief seethed round his pebble of a heart which by a miracle, continued to remain on the surface.

Sometimes Petatorov felt like eating, and he went to the nearest furniture shop—to earn a rouble or two, shifting luxury suites.

"I should telephone Nadya," thought Petatorov—"or telephone someone, but there's no one to telephone to, they're all busy with their own affairs. And a minute hope prevents me from dying; suddenly something might happen, and I'd begin to live differently. I don't dream of happiness—that's quite beyond me. I just want—to feel *different*. Everything's collapsed, nothing has remained, but the sharp splinters fly about and hit you in the face. A cheerful and energetic man may appear and open his umbrella and shout: This way!"

"Depression can wear you down, and then you feel grateful to that fascinating, cheerful, entertaining man. Then it's not important what he says—so long as he speaks with faith and hope. People follow him in serried ranks."

"But what *is* the way out? I won't leave it at that! I'm not a drunk, I'm Petatorov!"

He hurried home to Sokolniki.

I'm going to spend today sleeping. I must work! I'm not going to give myself up so easily, they won't catch me with their bare hands! After all, I realize a great deal, and I'll shout it out to people. I've earned the right to shout to everyone's face! And the frost is not important, nothing's important, the main thing is—to shout in time before all those fascinating, vigorous people have had time to mushroom everywhere! I'll sound the alarm, they will hear, they cannot fail to hear!

Petatorov opened the door—and saw his things: his mattress and books, dumped on the kitchen floor. Beside them lay a piece of paper. He picked it up and read the clumsy handwriting: "Philip! I called twice, but you were out. There's a job for you. Drop in any day in the morning. Yuli."

Behind the door of what used to be Petatorov's room could be heard half-drunken voices and female squeaks. The new lodgers were having a house-warming.

Chapter 7

The Cellars

The old woman crawled out.

"Phil, do forgive me, it just happened that way, I haven't any money, so I let them take it. And somehow you'll . . . manage . . ."

"No, I won't die," said Petatorov. "Just keep my things here, until I find another room, won't you?"

"Of course, Phil, it goes without saying, leave them . . . for the moment. Perhaps you'd like to sleep here tonight. I'll fix up something?"

"Don't worry, Ma, I'll find a place."

Petatorov went through the gate; the cat rushed headlong after him.

"Phil, have you been thrown out?!" she cried. "It's monstrous! That woman has no heart!"

"She has a heart, all right," Petatorov smiled wryly, "but she hasn't any money."

D

"It's inhuman! How am I going to live now? And there won't be anyone to talk to."

"It had to happen, Puss. The unpleasant thing is that it happened in winter—it's much too cold."

"Phil, what shall I do without you?"

The cat was running beside Petatorov.

"Come and visit me, Puss. I'll save some sausage specially for you. Come with Vaska . . ."

"But where are you going to live?"

"Near Taganka, probably . . ."

"Philikins, that's awfully far, I don't know the way there . . . Don't abandon me! The new lodgers are just drunks!"

They had reached the delicatessen on the corner.

"Farewell, Puss." The cat leaped on to Petatorov's shoulder and purred. Philip stroked her. The cat gave a sob, jumped down and dashed into a gateway.

"Well, and so I'm left to my own resources," thought Petatorov. "Tonight I'll sleep in the Kazan station, to-morrow I'll go to Taganka and find somewhere to live."

"It's cold . . . there's no snow—it's cold. The telegraph wires are covered with hoar frost, the streets are enmeshed in thin white strings, which vanish in sheaves into the darkness over the roofs. Trams clatter, there is a smell of burning in the air.

Petatorov reached the station and pushed his way through the crowd. On all sides he was surrounded by peasants carrying packs, but he deftly manœuvred in between monstrous bunches of pretzels and bagels. He found a place for himself on a bench and wrapped his head up with his scarf. Light filtered through—green, red, disturbing his doze, but he had to get himself accustomed to it. Locomotives whistled and pulled trains away to other towns—Petatorov did not care: there was no one he knew there, just different people with their worries—good luck to them. All around him people were making a noise, jabbering and munching rolls, telling each other what they had seen, why they had come and what they had bought.

   I'm all right with them. No one bothers me and I shall sleep. It's warm here, people are talking . . . it's peaceful . . .

—just out of it, from the Dvina. They put my son in prison—don't rightly know why—it wasn't him . . . but it's him they sentenced . . .
                              . . . I pleaded to have the case heard again, but they told me . . .
                         how much longer has he got?

well, they say, he's got three more months, and you're pleading

. . . that year, when they burnt down the police station back home . . .
. . . and so he'll come, so that

                                        so that

THE TRAIN IS LEAVING NO. 3 PLATFORM

                                        so that

—Ow, hee hee, ow! Stop it, Petka, hee-hee!

                      so that that that taht taht taht
take your foot away, bugger you

                                    so that
Phew!

why I've never been here before what street is this eh-eh
street! you hit him no really you don't say because he's
above all ethical the sistine madonna? but there's no
beer you're trash philip arkadyevich yessir, trash! trash

                                TRASH
                                    TRASH

"So that's what I said to her, there's no point going on
and on like that I'd better leave, but she kept yelling:
you've corrupted my daughter! I'll call the police, they'll
teach you to keep the moral code!
    they dragged me off she and the cop did and put me
in her bed go and live with her.

                                  so that

HEAD PORTER PIPIN YOU ARE WANTED AT THE
CONTROLLER'S OFFICE

                                  so that

I paid for it and that's that, if you had paid as much
I love you
you must hold your fork in the left hand

dearest
you must hold your fork in the left hand
do help me
fork in the left
kiss me
if you hold it in the left

can't say exactly that we lived badly. No, we had a bit
of an allotment, our own cabbage, potatoes, we used to
buy milk, so it wasn't bad, can't say it was bad. Only
something somehow nagged at me, and I didn't know what
it was, but it nagged and nagged as if I hadn't settled in
the right place and one day I says

for-ward march!

I shall simply call you Phil whatever you may discover
for nothing is important really, all one really wants to
do is to live and not merely to indulge in fantasies but
you indulge in fantasies you try to be too clever by half
but what good is that to anyone the armour of spon-
taneous clever dicks is made of the best steel

man became man because he began holding his fork in
his left hand

so that

THEY SHOT HIM BECAUSE HE BEHAVED DISGRACE-
FULLY AND HELD HIS FORK IN HIS RIGHT HAND
SWINE HE HELD HIS FORK THEREFORE THEY SHOT

HIM DO NOT DO WHAT OTHERS DO NOT DO IF
OTHERS START DOING IT THEN YOU TOO MAY
START DOING IT

                              SO THAT
                    Tha that! aaaaat!

don't be what you are but be the person people like
you will live forever in people's memory and have glory
eternal too if you behave well
            and we had cabbage and cucumbers something
nagged me for some reason

excuse me are *you* the author of the famous "Decent
Tragedy" I've admired you for a long time

moral principles thats the most important thing and don't
drink but because you can't drink beer by yourself when
everyone swoons with delight

                              GO ON, SWOON

THE MAIN THING IS TO SWOON IN TIME AND NOT TO DRINK
BEER BECAUSE EVERYONE IS SWOONING

BUT YOU ARE DRINKING BEER THIS IS A CHALLENGE TO
WORLD OPINION

HE WAS SHOT BECAUSE HE DRANK BEER AND DID NOT
SWOON

excuse me but I want some beer why can't I drink beer just think: why shouldn't I drink beer while you are swooning

go into it more deeply: why be in raptures when what prevents you doing so is the fact that you haven't drunk any beer for a long time and you terribly want to drink some

a classic example during his lifetime leo tolstoy used the letter o 1234554321 times

LEO TOLSTOY IS LEAVING PLATFORM THIRTEEN AT ZERO ZERO FOUR HOURS

glory to the joker of yasnaya polyana[1] for having been the first to realize that shakespeare was shit but not him because he was not shit

HEAD PORTER PIPIN THEY HAVE BEEN WAITING FOR YOU FOR A VERY LONG TIME AT THE CON-TROLLER'S OFFICE

"Hey, sailor!"

Petatorov was rudely woken by the charwoman's broom. The men were getting up and moving their stringed bagels to that half of the waiting-room which had already been washed. Petatorov exchanged a few

[1] i.e. Leo Tolstoy (*Tr. note*).

swear words with the charwomen, and then jumped up.

Off to Taganka, to find a temporary place to live. The harder life is, the lighter one's heart, the simpler and more understandable everything is.

He almost bought a meat pie, so intoxicated was he by its warm and nourishing smell, but he remembered himself in time.

. . . He was walking along the embankment, past factories and small houses.

Heavy trucks were stopping and emptying out snow into the river.

At the bridge, Petatorov turned left.

He was at home at last, on a little island of the free world; but this, too, had its prince—Mynia, a mechanic. It was he who was the father and benefactor[1] of the Taganka cellars. It was he who was the patron of down-at-heel artists and people without residence permits. The cellars cordially welcomed everyone, insisting only on no noise and that one should do what Mynia said. What Mynia usually said was: "Listen, I'm not at all well today . . ." And the person without a residence permit would offer the foreman mechanic some vodka. Mynia was not impertinent; if you treated him, he would come again in a month to six weeks. He warned people of possible raids by the police; then the cellars would be closed and people would wait. Usually, no one turned up; once a year or once in two years the inhabitants would listen, smiling cynically, to the swaggering knocks

---

[1] "Father and benefactor"—words frequently used to describe Stalin during his lifetime (*Tr. note*).

on the iron-bound doors accompanied by the slogan-like exclamation: "Hey! Who's there, come out!" Then the police would disappear and life would go on, normal and quiet, again.

Petatorov went downstairs and walked along a long corridor, past noisy central heating boilers. He saw the glimmer of an iron-clad door. Petatorov listened, then knocked: rat-a-tat tat rat-a-tat. There was silence behind the door, then, after a pause someone asked:

"Who's there?"

"Friend."

The door opened with a rumble.

"Phil!" said a bushy tramp all covered with hair, only his nose and ears showing. "You're always a welcome guest, etc., I've forgotten the rest. Come in, preacher, seeker after truth and happiness!"

His host banged the door to and, bending down, they went through into the inner apartment. A cosy room, full of rags; by the wall on the left stood a real bed with brass knobs, covered with a real blanket. Petatorov sat down at the table and gazed with a smile at his old friend. They called him the Jap, as he had once been a translator from the Japanese.

"I live for my own pleasure," the Jap liked to boast, "until I was twenty-two years old not a drop of beer had passed my lips. I studied and tried hard, but then I suddenly understood how one should live: I have a drink and lie here, dreaming. In summer I work, get masses of money, and then back here I come. In autumn and winter up till January you won't find me with a drop of meths, I only drink vodka from the grocer's. But then poverty forces me to use varnish. But in winter, too, I translate a lot, but again for my own pleasure—I like the ancient Japanese."

"Phil," said his host, "what do you intend to do?"

"I have come to ask for shelter."

"Nowhere to live?"

"I was renting a room, yesterday they threw me out—I hadn't paid."

"Oh well, to hell with them We'll do without them. There's still another room here; move in."

They went to look at the accommodation. Perfectly decent, a little dirtier than one might wish. Petatorov swept the floor. The Jap brought a cloth to wipe the walls. They dragged in three old orange boxes and placed them along the wall, underneath a large central heating pipe. The Jap generously gave Phil an old divan bolster—with its stuffing coming out—to put under his head.

"You can sleep like that today, and tomorrow you can bring a mattress and set yourself up for good. I've got a warm cellar, and the window's big. I have to hang up a curtain for the black-out—Mynia insists. We'll go to him tomorrow with half a bottle of vodka, we'll come to an agreement with him."

Back in the Jap's room, Philip wearily sank down into a rocking-chair. His host opened a bottle of wine and brought some freshly-cooked potatoes from the kitchen. They had a drink. The Jap was chewing his potato in a melancholy way, staring into the corner.

"Phil," he said, "on the whole I'm glad that you've settled in with me, but one thing worries me; you too, my dear fellow, have started to sink."

"I'm not sinking," said Petatorov. "I don't want to remain in the cellar for ever. About six weeks ago I met my wife—and realized I had to do something. Yulka Sheptunov has promised me some work, and I'll leave as soon as I have some money."

"Look out! It's not easy to get out of here—it's too peaceful, comforting. The fall of the intellectual started long ago, you're not the first, and nor was I—and I've been living in this cellar for over six years. It's better to lie down than to travel.''

The vegetation on the Jap's face had begun to stir; a potato disappeared into it. He took a swig from the bottle. There was a leaden film over his eyes; he got drunk quickly.

"Phil, listen to some poetry! You are . . . were . . . a philologist, you'll understand!

> A fisherman fell asleep in his boat,
> He had covered his feet with the sail.
> The current gently draws
> The boat towards the West.
> The sun is going down,
> A diamond sparkles
> On the fisherman's cheek.

I know masses of poetry . . . but I'm beginning to forget it . . .''

Someone knocked on the door, giving a prearranged signal.

"Open it, Phil!!! It's for me."

Petatorov went and, when he had undone the bolt, he saw a fat woman with a cheerfully thoughtless expression, standing on the threshold.

"He's here, come in," he said.

"Ah-ah-ah, you've come, smarty!" the Jap bellowed, and he belched out a stream of filthy curses. "Have you brought it?!"

"I have, you scarecrow!" The woman was no less skilfully abusive, but she did it with much more style. "Well, when are you going to kick the bucket, you parasite!"

"Not for a long time yet, smarty! Ha-ha!"

The woman took out a packet of cigarettes and a little bag. The Jap watched avidly: she shook out the tobacco and mixed it with a fine brown-coloured powder, filled the tube of the cigarette with the mixture, and held it out to the Jap—he was trembling with impatience.

"Light it up, you bitch!" he ordered in a choked whisper.

When the cigarette began to glow, the Jap inhaled with a chesty wheeze—and sprawled on the bed.

"Would you like a smoke?" the woman asked Petatorov and across her face—or perhaps it only seemed so? —there flashed a smile of hatred.

"No, I'd better be going."

The Jap roused himself. "Make yourself scarce, you son of a bitch. Don't let me set eyes on you, you linguist, or I'll thro-o-otle you! And . . . don't you touch my woman!!"

. . . Philip was lying down, feeling the wooden ribs of packing-cases through his thin coat.

Tomorrow I'll collect my mattress and books, and the day after tomorrow I'll go and see Yuli. Must get out of this, Phil, my dear prof. . . . But where is Nadyenka! My weakness has gone, I feel uncommon strength, I'll turn all the cellars . . . topsy-turvy.

am I asleep or not?

The blizzard is howling outside

I'm very frightened of blizzards

The howling, howling, whistling

Nadezhda!

What, darling?

Eh?

I love you

the blizzard moaoaoaoans!

hide me

tyup

tyup

tyup drip

tyup drip

tyup drip

tyup in

I am warm sleeping

O . . .! Sorry!

(Petatorov opened his eyes: the Jap stood beside him).

"When I drink, I can't bear to see anyone, makes me sick. Get up, lunch is ready."

Phil raised himself on his elbows, looked at the central-heating pipe, then at the Jap. He jumped down and walked about making a scratching noise with his toenails on the floor.

"Must drop in on Mynia," he said.

"We'll have a bite first, he can wait, the sot."

They ate some potatoes in the kitchen and chatted about the peculiarities of Japanese versification.

"The Japanese don't like long poems," said the Jap, munching an onion. "And they are absolutely right. They don't mind a thirty-one syllable stanza, they've realized that a poet can't speak uninterruptedly, and that if he does he's only filling in the spaces between the grains—They have preferred to collect golden grains.

Have you noticed that, in their poetry, there are no *bad* poems? In Europe for a long time the sonnet almost triumphed, but nevertheless the desire to write rhymed tomes carried the day. Their books appeal, not through the poems, but through the mystery of a poem. The *tanka* is the most beautiful of aphorisms, one admires it, whereas the European aphorism frightens and shocks."

"But what about Pushkin?"

"There's no family without one lucky member. And you know, Phil, joy appears in Europe only when something is being *overthrown*. There's very little of it, since we're not prone to affirmation, there's no joy, it's laughter that reigns: a television viewer's paunch heaving, full of cabbage soup . . .

They washed up and went to see Mynia.

Sparse, fine snow was falling and sprinkling the frail saplings in the little courtyard. A felt boot protruded from the crown of a slender poplar.

"There you are!" said the Jap with pride. "That's the symbol of the cellars' victory over society. One day two dim old women turned up, members of the self-same society since the year one thousand six hundred and ninety five, and started yelling: 'Hoolikans! parasites! Vat's the police about? Ve're koing to clean zings up here!' They beat up our Mynia, knocked out two of his teeth; meanwhile, we wrapped up the Actor—we've got one living here—in a sheet, and he lay down in the snow outside the door of the boiler-room. When they came out, the Actor was after them, sniggering, twittering, squealing: 'I'm Death, I'm aaafter yououou! Trotsky is dying of boredom in his cauldron without you!' They looked round—and took to their heels. The Actor was after them, after society. They ran and upset a trolley-bus into the Yauza river, the Actor didn't let up, he was squealing: 'You won't ge-e-t awaaaay, we'll cut lines on your skin! We'll write all the works of Mochetov[1] on you with a red-hot needle!' So society ran away. Next morning, so it is said, they arrived in Narofominsk, where they died singing the party anthem."

"Splendid!"

"We collected some money, Mynia had a new set of teeth, we poured out a fee for the Actor, and the felt boot was hoisted as a memorial to the joint struggle . . . This way!"

Mynia was sleeping in the boiler-house. The Jap gave him a shove, and said:

"Here's a new settler."

"Eh?" Mynia asked.

"Be introduced: a new lodger."

Mynia raised his head with difficulty and looked at Philip.

"Literally impossible."

"Mynia!"

"I don't feel well today." And he let his head fall back on his quilted jacket. The Jap took out the half-bottle of vodka and rubbed its smooth side against Mynia's hand. The mechanic felt the bottle with all five fingers, which then slid with it under his stomach.

"All ri. . . ." he said, his voice deadened by the quilted jacket. "Let him—"

In the little courtyard Petatorov took leave of the Jap and went off to fetch his mattress and books. His landlady handed him yet another note from Sheptunov.

"I called. You'll lose the job—where on earth have you got to?! Drop in as soon as you possibly can."

"Tomorrow," thought Petatorov. "What day is it to-morrow? *Thursday.*"

[1] It is suggested by the anonymous French translator that this is a dig at the Stalinist novelist Kochetov (*Nikto*, Paris, 1973, p. 145).

Chapter 8

The Break-up

On Thursday Petatorov did not manage to get to Sheptunov. He awoke at mid-day, it was warm and comfortable, he did not even feel hungry. And then he lay there, smoking and reading Homer. The Jap came, together with the Actor. The Actor had an ear missing. They were drinking tea, and the Actor was developing his theory: the lower a man sinks, the greater the heights of understanding he reaches. "With worries about comfort and daily bread you haven't time to think of the crux of the matter; truth is in understanding: once you have understood—don't undertake anything, otherwise you will suffer. All my life I played the Actor and I acquired a taste for it. Very content with little."

"Yes," said Petatorov, "but we are all so separated from each other, what is human about us?"

"That's how it has always been, and ever will be.

Everyone decides for himself on his own. One doesn't give a damn for the rest! Something unprecedented has occurred: a whole nation has been raped; perhaps, in some distant future, it will give birth to something—God forbid that it should be a Priapus, but meanwhile—keep quiet! You, Phil, aspire to be Christ, but no one asked Jesus about His residence permit and His nationality, no one expelled Him to Kilometre 101 beyond Jerusalem. He was allowed to say everything. But you—keep quiet!"

"I don't want to!"

"Then create, test, try! Only look out for your teeth, or you won't have anything to munch your rations with!"

"To a certain extent the Actor is right," remarked the Jap. "The human in you is screaming out, you're not a meek man. If you want to be happy, close your eyes, he-he!"

The Actor ran to fetch a bottle of wine, they had a drink. The Jap was telling them about an attack of D.T.'s.

"I arrived at the grocer's and saw everyone had wings on his back—snow-white wings. I was very frightened. They were all crowding round with their wings, even the local police inspector, who flew into the shop on wings. It was he who saved me. I'll never forget how he boxed my ears."

Someone knocked, giving a prearranged signal. The Jap got up and opened the door—it was his woman.

"If you're going to see a woman don't forget the antibiotics!" said the Actor, in a nasal tone. The Jap let out an oath and took the woman away to his room.

"I'm off," said the Actor. "I'll lie down a bit."

Petatorov stretched out on the packing-cases, smoked, and tried not to believe what the Actor had said.

He fell asleep—until morning; from time to time he heard the Jap's groans on the other side of the wall:

"Don't wriggle about, Smarty!!! What a fool you are! You can't even string two words of Japanese together . . ."

. . . .

"Hello, Philip! At last!" exclaimed Sheptunov joyfully. "You very nearly lost the job—and it's a splendid one."

"What kind of work is it?"

"I know someone at the top, Comrade Shulyatko, and this is what he proposes: you have to walk up and down the room with a metal object in your hands. Fee—a hundred roubles."

"That's the first I've heard of that perversion . . . Curious. And when?"

"This evening, if you like."

"Splendid! But what about having some tea?"

The cups were steaming. The friends were putting sugar in their tea and stirring it. Bitter-sweet tea.

"Yuli, this has cheered me up no end. I'm ready to throw bombs."

"Ah, Philip, you must first understand, and then you'll see things differently. I, for example, had some wine today . . . of course, that's not important . . . At the moment it's clear to me: we don't want to lick *their* bottoms. Art and all that is just a gilded beading in which they frame their own actual bottom. Peter[1] opened a window on to Europe, in order, apparently, that they might then exhibit their own imperishable bottoms in that same window."

"Keep to the point, Yuli."

"All right! Drink up your tea, Philip."

[1] Peter the Great (*Tr. note*).

Impatiently, Petatorov swallowed the hot liquid, without being aware of the taste.

"Let's go! Where's your Shulyatko?!"

". . . zee whole zing depends on diesels and fuel. Vee have zat fuel, but ze Americans haven't!"

"Because zey lag behind our tempos . . ."

. . . The trolleybus was very crowded. They were riding along a dark street, only intermittently lit by buzzing lights. The friends got out, and the wind spun round them, spattering them with finely chipped ice.

"It's here," said Sheptunov, and opened a door.

"Halt!" said someone enveloped in furniture fabric. "Where to?"

. . . .

The old man threw some pine-extract cubes into the bath and shuffled into his room to get the hour-glass. He glanced out of the window. Cold. The building opposite looked dead, with curtains covering its eye-sockets. Not so much as one little strip of light. A nasty chill crept inside him, and he went into the bathroom. Wonderful green water, smelling marvellously of pine planks. Afraid of slipping, he took a long time to climb into the bath. He stretched out his hand and turned over the hour-glass.

A fine trickle of sand flowed down.

. . . .

"Can we see Comrade Shulyatko?" Yuli asked a handsome, muscular young man.

"We've been expecting you for a long time!" said the young man with a French accent, smiling. "Please come in!"

They went into the flat accompanied by the sound of the rattling chain.

Shulyatko emerged to meet them.

"My friends! You've just arrived in time, I was already thinking of another candidate." He opened the door of the half-empty waiting-room. "Let us introduce ourselves."

"Philip Arkadyevich."

Shulyatko seized Petatorov's hand and squeezed it gently:

"How very, very nice! Yuli, ten for you . . . as we agreed . . ."

"Raymond!" Shulyatko called. "See Yuli out. Yes, by the way my good fellow, do telephone in a week's time and get some new goods ready for me . . ."

When Raymond had led Sheptunov away, Comrade Shulyatko explained:

"That young chap is doing a course with me . . ."

He took a little key on a silk ribbon from round his neck and winked at Petatorov.

"We'll start at once!" And he sniggered.

The professor was bursting with curiosity; he watched Shulyatko unlocking a little door in the wall.

What makes these people tick? This is the first time I'm in high society. And what in general do they know and want to know about us? If one were to say to them, as one man to another: wait a bit, stop breaking people for a moment, let others have a say too. A few more years will pass, and again blood will flow . . .

"This way, please, Philip Arkadyevich!"

Shulyatko pressed a button. A deep reddish-violet light filled the room.

Petatorov was dumbfounded. Garlands of chains and fetters, rings, manacles, ancient chipped axes, whips, knives, tongs, were hanging on the walls, glimmering dimly. A rack stood in one corner, while in another there was a carpenter's bench with vices screwed on to it, and heaped with instruments. Low, soft armchairs leaned lazily backwards.

"I'll explain everything," said Shulyatko, seeing Petatorov's amazement. "As you know, I am a person of national importance, I get very tired—after all, we have so many worries! But this room here is my rest room, so to speak. As Karl Marx said: "Nothing human is alien to me."[1] You understand, of course, that this should not be spread around: rumours, gossip, might start, and people like us in the government must be on our guard—they're all trying to catch each other out! One comes home tired —enough to hang oneself, but then I stroke these chains, or crack a whip, and strength comes back from goodness knows where, hee-hee! Or else I make a few fetters—I made all this myself, except for a few very rare specimens. It took me a year and a half to make the rack. And just look at this: a garotte with a clockwork mechanism—a man can be strangled gradually for two whole hours! I feel that I'm a real Kulibin[2]—but I'm not going to take the bread out of people's mouths. Anyway I myself know that I'm an expert. Hey-hey! But now, my good fellow, allow me to put these on you . . ."

Shulyatko clicked the locks of the handcuffs.

"And now this one . . ." He deftly hobbled Petatorov with fetters and tied a long chain to his belt. He stood back and admired his work, and began to breathe very fast.

[1] *"Nihil humanum a me alienum puto"* (Terence) (*Tr. note*).
[2] Russian self-taught engineer and clock-maker, 1735–1818 (*Tr. note*).

"That's good!" he whispered, stepping backwards towards an armchair. "Go on, walk, walk, that's all you've got to do!" And he fell back into the plush arms.

The professor took a step—uncertainly and clumsily, the chains jangled, and clanked.

"Ah!" yelped Shulyatko and flopped back in his chair.

. . . .

Petatorov was floating in a red haze, clanking his chains, while the hulk of Comrade Shulyatko was growing and swelling, filling the whole room, and ousting what remained of the air.

"Here they are, my little dears! Tra-ha-ha! I've got you all right, here in my fist! I've crushed you?—too bad, ha-ha! Crowds are trailing along, and trees stand all around and . . . dogs! We'll have you where we want you. There won't be a squeak from you. I, I am your lord and master!!! Weeping, are you? Thinking of your wives and children? And what am I here for?! To use whips and tongs on you all, I'll cut your flesh up into segments! You'll tremble all right and groan, and your bones will crunch in my fist!! A-a-a-a, marvellous! Ah, ah, ah, ah. Bliss, bliss! Oh! He's crying, groaning is he, all right then, I'll pour some molten lead down his gullet, ah! ah-ah! Poetry. . . read some poetry . . . about suffering! . . ." gasped Shulyatko, slithering down the armchair.

Petatorov heard him, and began mumbling as he went round the room in circles:

> Straight lies the railroad with
> narrow slopes banking it,

Bridges and fence-posts and rails,
And, all along, there are Russian
bones flanking it
Many, how many . . .[1]

"Yes that's just it! Russian bones! what a clanging of chains! and that's how they marched, and they are still marching like that: dingdong—ding-dong—dingdong! A hundred! A thousand! Three hundred billion!!!! and *I* —I am the boss! And their flesh is sizzling in the flame! ah, ah, ah! that's Shulyatko for you! Ah! Ah! Bliss, bliss!"

Shulyatko grasped the arms of the chair, occasionally he gave a shudder, his face flushed with fire, and every cell of his body was singing a song of happiness. Physical ecstasy was bearing him aloft, everything grew bright, people in chains were shouting and sobbing, jingling their fetters, and dying with curses on their lips. Flesh was smoking, Shulyatko's nostrils were quivering, taking in all the smells of pain and terror.

. . . now a clamour arose, oh so threatening! Menacing!
Tramping and gnashing of teeth
Frost-covered windows were crossed by a shadow . . .
Who's there? A crowd of the dead.[1]

"Is that really true?" thought the professor, choking, and forgetful of where he was—his whole life and all Russia was passing before his eyes. "There it is, *my life*, and I never suspected it. I wanted to seek, I cherished the hope that I would invent happiness. The recipe for happiness was iretrievably lost long ago. If one man is happy, another is cursing the world. There's no happiness, only

---

[1] From N. A. Nekrasov's poem, *The railroad* (1864) (*Tr. note*).

a pair of scales. And to whom did I want to shout? The towers have no red stars on them,[1] my dear cockroaches, but hands of clay making rude signs. May you be damned! . . ."

Shulyatko was quite beyond himself. Pleasure had drained him, his face was running with sweat, which was washing away his voluptuous smile. Shulyatko oozed off his chair, his head came rolling after the rubber tube of his neck, and with a dull, wooden thud bounced on the parquet. With difficulty his hand felt for a secret bell, and pressed it.

. . . The professor looked at Raymond's handsome face with amazement; the latter swiftly removed the fetters and handcuffs and led Petatorov out into the corridor.

"That's for your work," said the Frenchman, pleasantly rolling his "r's", and slipped an envelope into the professor's pocket. "I'll see you out."

Petatorov submitted to the shoving of a strong, young hand; he concentrated on his thoughts and was soaring over the scorched field of his life.

Clasping Raymond's arm, he went down the staircase.

. . . .

The old man felt warmer now and lost himself in his day-dream. His eyes wandered affectionately over the walls and the ceiling, and suddenly caught sight of the hour-glass. "Good Lord! I've been sitting here too long!" All the sand had run into the lower bubble of the hour-glass, and lay there in a little pointed mound. The old man, alarmed, quickly got out of the water, which smelt pleasantly of planks, and wrapped himself up in a Turkish towel. He padded into the bedroom and drank a cup of

[1] Reference to the five-pointed stars, emblems, of the USSR, on the Kremlin towers (*Tr. note*).

prepared medicine. He went to the window and glanced into the black pit of the alleyway. Br-r! There stood the house opposite, gloomy and without sign of movement. A single bulb was burning over the entrance. The old man saw the door open and someone push a man out into the street. The man ran a few steps and fell. He got up, swaying, but regained his balance, and wandered off down the alleyway.

"One of *their* poor relations has swilled down too much liquor, the swine!" thought the old man with distaste, and drew the curtain.

Chapter 9

Night

Petatorov was going home to his cellar. Flashing fragments of sentences were flying through his mind, he had forgotten that he had some money and that he could have taken a taxi—he was going back on foot. He successfully dragged himself as far as the embankment, stopping from time to time and sitting on a snow-drift, where he would rest and think. The professor rubbed snow on his face, which was burning, and he found it difficult to seize on any thought, to hang on to it, and not to fall. He turned a corner and stumbled. A gust of wind flew up, trying to help the professor to get to his feet, and rushed away. Petatorov crawled after it, leaving behind him a broad band of trampled-down snow.

Where am I . . . Ah, my beloved cellar, so I'm back home no it's the little garden! the garden why is it under snow while I'm too hot . . . trees you say Christ didn't have a residence permit for Jerusalem! Oh, there are people around me! They are the disciples. Don't sleep tonight, will you? Watch with me. Today I speak unto you. You, my neighbour, bend down that I may kiss you—my brother . . .

Petatorov's lips touched the frozen crust of snow.

Thank you. I have cooled them. Now this is what I want . . .

Remember that you are men, do not allow yourselves to lie. Corruption has penetrated into every pore, with a stench have you stifled your spirits.

Trample not upon your diamond, for how then shall you differ from the beasts?

Man cannot live alone, do not forget mankind!

Even I cannot atone for your guilt, there is no cry which can wrest your servitude from you.

Go now and preach this, even though they may mock you and insult you.

Infect them with goodness, even as others have infected them with fear.

But dare not to speak before you have faith.

Curse yourselves and be filled with despair, and then shall you see it, the golden nugget of your soul in your very depths.

Lest you cease to live like men.

. . . and behold! you my disciples, have fallen asleep. You are weary, this is tedious for you, for you have long *known* this . . .

Petatorov fell face downwards on the snow and cried out: "Oh Lord! No one will hear me. Oh Lord!"

He clawed the snow and crawled—falling over, choking—to the doors of the cellar; down the steps he went with the aid of his hands—down, very slowly. His body swept away the dust and refuse from the concrete floor— on he went, towards the shiny armour-plating of the iron door of paradise.

He jerked his body up and, turning the key in the lock with his teeth, hung there.

Here is paradise at last, warm and quiet. I'll lie down straight away, I'll have a drink of wine . . .

Petatorov climbed on to the packing-cases and stretched out, his eyes came to rest on a big heating-pipe—rusty, with yellow patches. It hung over him, and its heat penetrated his body, and his heart was filled with sweetness. He rummaged round the head of his bed—a bottle. He took a sip and spat it out—what a bitter taste! Vinegar.

And suddenly the professor noticed that the pipe had started descending. He looked more closely: it was, indeed, coming down, very, very, slowly. Now he could reach it without getting up. He touched the pipe's surface: it was burning hot, the plaster stank.

In a moment it'll be quite warm . . . that's enough, my dear pipe, or it'll be too hot.

The pipe came down still further, rested on his chest, and an unbearable weight fell on Petatorov. He pressed his hands against the pipe, it was becoming heavier and heavier, he could not move the burden or slip out from under it. He heard the plywood boxes under him cracking; as it settled, the pipe pressed into his chest.

The crates are cracking! They're flimsy. How did they manage to come all the way from Africa . . .

Petatorov was transfixed by pain, he twitched, and the sound of a cry reached him:

" . . . iiiliii! . . . iiiliii! . . ."

Swift light little feet were running just above the

window and again he heard the sound of the beloved voice: "Philip!" and then, far away by then:

"iiiliiii! . . ."

"Nadezhda!" Petatorov wanted to reply, but only a rattle escaped from his throat, followed by a flow of hot blood. He choked; and then he heard the trumpets begin to sound, and the drums to beat.

Phil we are dying

tatata

    tatata—taaa—a

        ta ta

          TA TA

            TAT TA TA TA

the bells!

the bells are ringing!

bam bam bam bam bam bam bam bam bam bam bam
mm mmm mmm mmm mmm mm mmm mmm mmm mmm

BAMMM

BAMMM   BAMMM

BAMMM

The police cars drove into the courtyard with their lights out. Here and there, the windows of the cellars, no wider than a pair of hands, were lit up. The building was sinking into the ground and several stories had already collapsed. Mynia had warned the inhabitants of a possible raid, and in the courtyard an aged grandfather in a short fox-fur jacket stood guard. He gave a penetrating whistle and disappeared into the boiler-house. The lights in the cellars immediately went out.

"What do you want us to do, Captain?" asked a freckled sergeant, who was always laughing.

"Flush them out," said the captain, gloomily.

"Yes, sir."

Vigorous fists began knocking on doors, broken glass tinkled.

"Op-en up!"

They broke a window, the light of a torch searched the walls and came to rest on a man, he was lying on some packing-cases, his head was hanging down un-naturally—just as if the neck were broken—his face turned towards the window. Seeing the happy smile on the greyish-pale face and the blood on the cheeks and chin, the sergeant gave a start. He reported to the captain, picked up a long, pointed plank and pushed it through a chink in the window. For a long time he

carefully prodded the man's stomach, then the shoulders,
and then pushed the body on to the floor.

The man did not stir.

1966.

THE LIBERATING BOND

COVENANTS – BIBLICAL AND CONTEMPORARY

Wolfgang Roth
Rosemary Radford Ruether

USE GUIDE

by Elizabeth L. McWhorter

Friendship Press • New York